HAMBURGER

Edible

Series Editor: Andrew F. Smith

EDIBLE is a revolutionary new series of books dedicated to food and drink that explores the rich history of cuisine. Each book reveals the global history and culture of one type of food or beverage.

Already published

Pancake Ken Albala

Pizza Carol Helstosky

Forthcoming

Spices Fred Czarra

Pie Janet Clarkson

Beer Peter La France

Cake Nicola Humble

Caviar Nicola Fletcher

Chocolate Sarah Moss

Cocktails Joseph M. Carlin

Curry Colleen Taylor Sen

Fish and Chips Panikos Panayi

Hot Dog Bruce Kraig

Lobster Elisabeth Townsend

Tea Helen Saberi

Tomato Deborah A. Duchon

Hamburger

A Global History

Andrew F. Smith

REAKTION BOOKS

Published by Reaktion Books Ltd
33 Great Sutton Street
London EC1V ODX
www.reaktionbooks.co.uk

First published 2008

Printed and bound in China by C&C Offset Printing Co., Ltd

British Library Cataloguing in Publication Data

Smith, Andrew F. (Andrew Franklin), 1946–
Hamburger : a global history. – (Edible)
1. Hamburgers
2. Hamburgers – History
I. Title
641.8'4

ISBN-13: 978 1 86189 390 1

Contents

Introduction

My first recollection of eating away from home was at a little hamburger stand across the street from a park in Sunland, California, where I spent my early years. Fifty-eight years later I can still remember the portly elderly proprietor, his white apron splotched with grease, ketchup and mustard. His compact lunch wagon, fitted with a grill for cooking the beef patties, was hardly big enough to contain his bulk. I don't recall side orders, cold drinks, desserts or French fries – just the hamburgers. Our family always ordered five hamburgers, at a total cost of one dollar – quite a bargain in 1950. As far as I can remember, we were his only customers, which was just as well because he took at least ten minutes to cook, garnish and wrap our burgers. When you're four years old and hungry, ten minutes can be an eternity. We ate in the car or at picnic bench, and then ran back to play in the park.

My memories of the neighbourhood hamburger vendor were eclipsed five years later by my first visit to McDonald's. Compared with the little cart in the park, McDonald's was a dazzling palace. The building was clean, spacious, colourful and brightly lit. Through the forward-tilting glass façade where we placed our order, the staff – clean-cut teenage boys

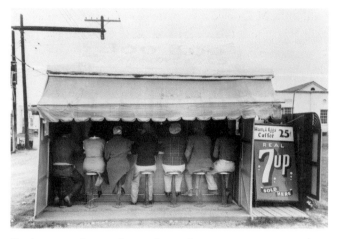

Hamburger stands were often outdoors, where customers were covered only with an awning, such as the one above in Harlingen, Texas, 1939.

– could be seen going about their tasks with quasi-military precision. There were lots of people queuing but service was speedy and the waiting time was brief. The menu was very limited – hamburgers, cheeseburgers, French fries, malts or fizzy drinks – but it was exactly what the customers wanted. What's more, the food was cheap: you could get an entire meal for less than 50 cents, and a family of four could be reasonably sated for under three dollars.

The billboard outside proudly announced that Mc-Donald's had sold over a million hamburgers. To me, this was simply an unimaginable quantity and, frankly, I didn't believe it. At the time, McDonald's had just started franchising, and there were only a dozen or so outlets in the Los Angeles area. It was inconceivable that such a small chain could have served so many burgers in such a short time.

Times have changed, and so has my perception of McDonald's. Sixty years after its founding, in 1948, as a small octagonal restaurant on E Street in San Bernardino,

California, McDonald's is a massive multinational conglomerate with more than 30,000 restaurants and an estimated 250,000 employees worldwide. Their signs now boast that they have sold more than 100 billion hamburgers, which works out to about sixteen burgers for every person alive in the world today.

The hamburger sandwich first appeared in the United States as a minor street food in the late nineteenth century. Within just a few decades the succulent sandwich became the focus of a whole new food distribution model: the 'fast-food' industry, which revolutionized the way Americans ate. From its birthplace, the hamburger was introduced to other countries, and by the late twentieth century it was the foundation of one of the fastest-growing businesses in the world.

The hamburger's rise to global prominence is a lively story, peopled with short-order cooks and top-flight chefs, street vendors and captains of industry, family-run diners and massive conglomerates, burger barons and vegetarians,

Interior of a small hamburger stand in the 1930s, Alpine, Texas, 1939.

hard-hitting advertisers and health-food advocates, fast-food freaks and 'slow-food' purists, hard-nosed critics and flavour-conscious aficionados. The hamburger sandwich has achieved this success through its adaptability to local cultures and tastes, and in the process it has changed the world.

Hamburger Fakelore

Like so many other matters related to culinary history, the hamburger's origins are shrouded in 'fakelore'. The Tartars had nothing to do with the hamburger; the citizens of Hamburg, Germany, had only a remote connection with the sandwich. There are several contenders for the title of 'inventor' of the hamburger sandwich, but no primary evidence has surfaced to support any of their claims. The frequently cited Delmonico's menu, dated 1834 and featuring 'Hamburg Steak', is a fake. The oft-quoted 1904 newspaper story about the hamburger vendor at the Louis and Clark Exposition in St Louis who supposedly invented the hamburger sandwich has not been identified, and even if it were, it would clearly not be the first instance of a hamburger sandwich in America. Ray Kroc did not found McDonald's and the first McDonald's restaurant was not in Des Plaines, Illinois.

I

Humble Hamburger Beginnings

In November 2006, Representative Betty Brown introduced a resolution into the Texas Legislature that formally designated Athens, Texas, as the 'Original Home of the Hamburger'. She based her resolution on the belief that Fletcher Davis had invented the hamburger at his lunch counter in Athens sometime during the 1880s. Hearings were held on this resolution, and it passed the Texas legislature in March 2007. Not to be outdone, the Wisconsin state legislature passed a resolution in August 2007 proclaiming Charlie Nagreen as the inventor of the hamburger and the town of Seymour as the real 'Home of the Hamburger'. Other prominent contenders who have been proclaimed inventors of the hamburger include the brothers Frank and Charles Menches, who reportedly served up the first burger sandwich in 1885 at the Erie County Fair in New York, and Louis Lassen of New Haven, Connecticut, who is credited for doing so around 1900.

Each of these cases has one thing in common – no primary evidence has surfaced to support its claims. Who really invented the hamburger sandwich – strictly defined as a hot ground-beef patty served between two pieces of bread – will probably never be known, but what is clear is that this combination arrived late in the nineteenth century, long after the invention of the sandwich and of the ground-beef patty.

The Invention of the Sandwich

The hamburger's remote roots date back to eighteenth-century England, the supposed birthplace of the sandwich. In the 1760s a Frenchman, Pierre-Jean Grosley, visited London and, upon his return to France, wrote about his experiences. His book became the most popular eighteenth-century travel guide to London. In it Grosley recounted how a minister of state had played cards for 24 hours straight, sustaining himself by eating only beef between two pieces of bread. Grosley claimed that this 'dish' was named for the ministerial gambling fiend. Grosley did not name the dish or identify its inventor, but Edward Gibbon, future author of *The History of the Decline and Fall of the Roman Empire*, reported in his journal that he had eaten a 'Sandwich' at the Cocoa-Tree, a fashionable gentlemen's gaming club, on 24 November 1762. Place these two sources together and the inventor of the dish would appear to be John Montagu, the Fourth Earl of Sandwich, who served as Minister of the Admiralty during the 1760s. In fact, the Earl is unlikely to have been the first person to consume a slice of beef between two slices of bread, but he has nevertheless been credited with the creation of the sandwich ever since.

Whatever its origin, the sandwich was simple to make and easy to eat. Its convenience contributed to its success. So did its taste: its multi-layers provided a vehicle for a diversity of flavours and textures, while its main components, such as bread and beef, remained relatively discrete. The sandwich first became fashionable in English high society.

By the 1770s, recipes for sandwiches appeared in English cookbooks and by the early nineteenth century similar recipes appeared in the United States. Most recipes instructed that sandwiches be constructed of very thin slices of bread, day-old sponge cakes or small rolls cut into bite-sized squares or triangles. Suggested fillings included cheese, ham, shrimp, oysters, potted meats, crabs, lobster, prawns, sausages, tongue, anchovies and poultry. These dainty pieces were served by hostesses at luncheons, teas, suppers and picnics, packed in baskets for the convenience of travellers, and were also sold in tea rooms. The little sandwiches were served on a platter; since they were small enough to be eaten whole, there was no need for individual plates.

In the United States, the sandwich travelled in a different direction. Diminutive sandwiches were served in upper-class households, but the working classes demanded heartier, more varied and substantial sandwiches made on large rolls. These sandwiches were often served at taverns and bars. A British observer, describing American bar counters in 1880, reported that they were loaded with huge piles of mammoth beef sandwiches, one of which, he claimed, was sufficient for a full meal. He was amazed to see how quickly they were consumed. These sandwiches were often given away in bars in the hope that the free lunch would encourage the customers to buy more drinks.

Beef was used as a sandwich filling from the very beginning, and recipes for thinly sliced beef and mustard sandwiches appeared in many cookbooks. Popular as they were, beef sandwiches were not for everyone. Even thin slices of meat in soft bread could be difficult to chew, particularly for individuals who had few or no teeth – a not-uncommon condition in the nineteenth century. Neither could people with poor digestion eat sliced or even chopped beef. Medical

13

professionals in Europe and the United States recommended raw beef for patients with digestive problems, a very common complaint in the nineteenth century. Raw lean beef was finely chopped and spread on bread, or its juices were extracted, heated and served as 'beef tea'. By the 1870s, recipes for raw scraped beef were published and thereafter appeared in European and American cookbooks, such as Elizabeth S. Miller's *In the Kitchen* (1875). In *The Boston Cooking School Cook Book* (1887) Mary J. Lincoln wrote that raw beef sandwiches might be found more palatable if toasted. A better way of serving raw beef, Steak Tartare, appeared on restaurant menus and in British cookbooks, such as ones by Charles Herman Senn, *Recherché Side Dishes* (1901) (see p. 127).

In 1867 a New York physician, James H. Salisbury, spoke out against eating raw beef, which he and other medical professionals believed caused disease. Salisbury suggested as an alternative that the scraped beef should be pressed into patties about an inch thick and grilled. He recommended adding condiments such as butter, pepper, salt, Worcestershire sauce, mustard, horseradish or lemon juice, if desired (see p. 126). By 1889, recipes for 'Salisbury Steak' appeared in medical works and in cookbooks. Similar recipes appeared under other names, such as the more common phrase 'Hamburg steak', which became prevalent during the late nineteenth century. The name 'Salisbury steak' did not become popular on menus until World War 1, when the German-sounding term was replaced with patriotic alternatives. Under any name, these beef patties were served on a plate and eaten with a knife and fork.

The difficulty in preparing these steaks was the laborious process of scraping the raw beef. The popularization of the meat grinder made this job infinitely easier. Although home-made meat grinders had existed since at least the 1840s and commercial grinders had been sold since the 1850s, they were not common in American households. When meat grinders were featured at the Philadelphia Centennial Exposition in 1876, they quickly became a kitchen necessity. Commercial meat grinders such as the Enterprise Chopper and the American Chopper became popular. By the 1880s, medical professionals, including Dr Salisbury, publicly endorsed the American Chopper for making medicinal beef preparations. Endorsements from chefs and cookery teachers soon followed.

The meat grinder was a great asset to butchers, who could now use unsaleable or undesirable scraps and organ meats that might otherwise have been tossed out. It also became possible to add non-meat ingredients to the ground beef, and it was very hard for the consumer to know what was actually in the mixture. Ground meat was cheap, ideal to sell to the working classes, and by adding even cheaper fillers, such as gristle, skin and excess fat, the butcher could enhance his already substantial profit.

Hamburg Beef

Real Hamburg beef was an expensive gourmet food in the nineteenth century. In theory it was a product from cows raised in the countryside around Hamburg, Germany, where it was prepared in many ways. One common way to prepare fresh Hamburg beef was to chop it, season it and form it into patties, but it would have to be used immediately. Prior to the advent of freezers, beef had to be preserved in other ways: it could be smoked, dried, salted or made into spiced sausages. As Hamburg beef was expensive outside northern Germany, recipes for making these patties with any type of beef were published in many nineteenth-century cookbooks. Beef patties became common throughout Europe, Great Britain and North America under a variety of names. In England and the United States, they were called chopped, minced or scraped beef patties, beef cakes, beefsteak cakes and sausage-meat cakes. The beef was frequently combined with other chopped meat, such as pork and lamb. Onions, garlic, salt and pepper were common patty seasonings. The patty was sometimes served raw but was more usually grilled or fried.

Germans had migrated to America since the seventeenth century, establishing communities in many regions, particularly in Pennsylvania. After the failed revolution of 1848, German refugees poured into major American cities, including New York, Philadelphia, Milwaukee, Cincinnati, St Louis and Chicago. Then, as now, one of the few areas of employment open to immigrants in cities was the food business. Many German immigrants worked on farms, while their urban cousins opened butcher shops, restaurants and delicatessens. By the late 1860s, German restaurants attracted a wide variety of patrons who were enticed by the tasty and inexpensive foreign food.

Hamburg steak first appeared on the menus of German restaurants in America during the early 1870s. Auguste Ermisch's restaurant in New York, for example, served Hamburger steak in 1873. According to a *New York Times* article, it was 'simply a beefsteak redeemed from its original toughness by being mashed into mincemeat and then formed into a conglomerated mass. This is very appetizing, but conscience compels us to state that it is inferior to the genuine article, which can also be had here in a very satisfactory condition of tenderness.' Hamburg steak was an inexpensive dish made by grinding beef not otherwise used for choice cuts, such as porterhouse or sirloin steak.

The name Hamburg steak would not have sounded unusual to the average American consumer. There were already familiar American foods named after European cities, including frankfurters (from Frankfurt), wieners (from Vienna) and Hamburg sausage (Hamburg). 'Hamburg steak' sounded much more elegant than 'ground beef'. It combined the cachet of foreignness with a word denoting a fine cut of quality beef. That it only cost eight or ten cents was a bonus. From the restaurateur's viewpoint, the dish was made with scraps that would otherwise have been used to make sausages or stocks. With commercial meat grinders readily available by the 1870s, Hamburg steak was easy and cheap to prepare and, properly seasoned, quite delicious.

Hamburg steak might well have remained just one item on the menu of cheap German eateries had it not been for Philadelphia's Centennial Exposition, held in 1876. During the six months that the Exposition was open, more than ten million visitors viewed the exhibits and ate at the restaurants, one of which, a German restaurant, was sponsored by Philip J. Lauber of Philadelphia. Lauber had paid the hefty sum of $6,000 for the right to construct a German restaurant at the fair, and then paid the astronomical sum of $56,000 to build a two-storey facility with a large tented courtyard in the middle. The restaurant featured German bands, German food and German beer and wine. It could accommodate 1,200 customers simultaneously, and the service was fast and efficient. Even though Lauber's restaurant burned down before the Exposition ended, it was still identified as the most successful restaurant at the fair. Thousands of customers dined at Lauber's daily. According to a contemporary article in the *New York Tribune*, one of the more popular items was Hamburg steak.

The Philadelphia fair gave the Hamburg steak wide visibility. By the 1880s the dish was appearing on menus of non-German restaurants and cookbooks contained recipes for it. Newspapers reported on this new delicacy, often describing how it was made. In 1887, for instance, the *Chicago Tribune* noted that Hamburg steak was 'made by chopping any lean piece of beef and cooking it with onions or garlic'. In North Dakota, the *Bismark Tribune* claimed that this new dish was prepared by a German meat market proprietor and that the concept was imported from New York. In 1889 Jessup Whitehead, the English-born Chicago restaurateur and author, wrote that Hamburg steak consisted of 'beef sausage meat containing minced onion and a slight flavor of garlic, formed in flat round pats and fried in butter; served either as plain steak for breakfast, or with various sauces as a dinner entrée'.

The Hamburg steak patty was often served with onions, gravy, mashed potatoes or French fries and vegetables. By 1900 it was a common dish in most restaurants in the United States, but was still served on a plate and eaten with a knife and fork.

The Invention of the Hamburger Sandwich

The Hamburg steak's leap from plate to sandwich was a simple one that seems inevitable from today's perspective. But it took almost two decades before the sandwich met the Hamburg steak. The invention of the hamburger sandwich was fostered by the industrialization of America. In the late nineteenth century, factories sprang up around many cities, particularly in New England, the middle states and the Midwest. Workers usually lived some distance from the newly constructed factories, and it was impossible for them to go home for lunch or dinner, as they had in the past. Workers often carried their meals to work with them, but other types of food service were developed to meet this need. Some large factories, for instance, opened cafeterias.

During the day, workers could go to grocery outlets, or visit street vendors on their way to or from work. However, as industrialization spread, many factories began operating at night. As virtually all groceries, cafeterias and restaurants closed in the early evening, feeding the night shift was a particular problem. The lack of food also affected other people who happened to be out at night. Walter Scott of Providence, Rhode Island, wisely saw this as an opportunity. In 1872, he constructed a handcart (subsequently converted into the popular Pioneer Lunch Wagon) and filled it with sandwiches, boiled eggs, buttered bread, pies and coffee. At around 8 p.m. he'd park it outside the local newspaper-printing plant, which operated through the night, and sat inside waiting for customers. Workers would come out to the cart, order and receive their food through a side window, and either eat their meal standing nearby or take it elsewhere.

Another Providence entrepreneur, Ruel B. Jones, saw Scott's success and decided that with a larger lunch cart he could sell more food and of course make more money. The larger wagon was successful and by 1887 Jones had acquired several of them, which he moved to different locations in the city, according to the proximity of potential customers. Other proprietors saw this success and began operating in Providence and other cities. In Worcester, Massachusetts, Sam Jones, Ruel's nephew, constructed a 'lunch wagon' with a complete kitchen. This caused a stir, and a boom in the construction of lunch wagons ensued. They were variously called 'fancy night cafés', 'night lunch wagons' and 'owl lunch wagons'.

Unlike previous models, the new lunch wagons had gas grills so they could serve hot food. One favourite food served by street vendors was the sausage, also called the frankfurter or wiener in America. As these were hard to eat standing up without plates and utensils, placing them in a bun made sense. By the 1870s, special frankfurter buns were being manufactured. Sausages in buns became popular at fairs, amusement parks, sporting events and other large gatherings. They were simple to make, cheap to buy and easy to eat. The composition of the sausages was frequently questioned, and some suggested that the cheap wieners were made from dog meat. Yale students began calling the night wagons 'dog wagons' and the term 'hot dog' had emerged by the 1890s.

Another product served in lunch wagons was Hamburg steak. Like the sausage, it consisted of ground meat but, unlike the sausage, Hamburg steak was made from fresh, raw meat which needed to be heated before it could be served. When lunch wagons began heating food on grills, Hamburg steak was a logical addition to the menu. Because many customers ate their food standing up, placing the beef patty in a bun made sense. Who was the first lunch wagon proprietor to sell the Hamburg steak between two pieces of bread is unknown, but, by the 1890s, it had already become an American classic. Reports of the 'hamburger steak sandwich' appear in newspaper accounts in far-flung places. In Reno, Nevada, the *Evening Gazette* reported in 1893 that 'Tom Fraker's celebrated Hamburger steak sandwiches are always on hand to replenish an empty stomach and even fortify Satan himself'. In Chicago, an article in the *Tribune* reported: 'A distinguished favorite, only five cents, is Hamburger steak sandwich, the meat for which is kept ready in small patties and cooked while you wait on a gasoline range.' In Los

Even small hamburger stands usually had booths, such as the one above in Alpine, Texas, 1939.

Angeles the hamburger was defined as 'a sandwich with a filling of chipped meat and onions'. Hamburgers were even enjoyed in Hawaii before the islands were annexed by the United States.

As hamburgers grew in popularity, lunch wagons sold as many as 400 in a day. In Decatur, Illinois, the local paper recorded that hamburger stands were 'legion' and that, late at night, the vendor was 'the busiest man in town'. The article went on to estimate that 25,000 hamburgers were sold in Decatur during a single day in 1902. Restaurants began serving hamburger sandwiches, and recipes for making them were published in mainstream cookbooks by the 1910s, although they did not commonly appear until the 1920s and '30s.

Early recipes reflected the variety of ways that hamburgers were made at the time. Eva Greene Fuller's recipe for 'Hamburger Steak Sandwich', published in *The Up-to-date Sandwich Book* (1927), makes no mention of a beef patty – only fried ground hamburger (see p. 127). Florence A. Cowles, who

An apron-clad woman cooks hamburgers in the kitchen. Milwaukee, Wisconsin, 1950.

published three sandwich books, included six recipes for 'Hamburg' sandwiches in her 1929 work. In many of these recipes the ground beef was not shaped into patties, but spread on buttered bread. When her book was published in England, however, all of the recipes for hamburger sandwiches were removed by the editors.

By the early twentieth century, the term 'hamburger sandwich' had been shortened to 'hamburger', or just 'burger'. By the 1920s, hamburgers began to be mentioned in American literature, such as Sinclair Lewis's *Arrowsmith* and *Free Air*. Indeed, by then hamburgers were also served in school cafeterias, where they were promoted as 'good, wholesome food, food which would be nourishing and satisfying, and yet not heavy'. And, what's more, kids liked them.

Hamburgers also became a staple food in the American home. They were easy to make in frying pans or in ovens with grills. Hamburgers became a staple of picnics, with outdoor barbecue pits used to cook the meat. When home barbecue grills became fashionable, hamburgers became part of summer fare. They were particularly associated with the American holidays of Memorial Day, Independence Day and Labor Day.

Hamburger Problems

The hamburger's road to glory was not always smooth. Vendors frequently overcooked the beef, resulting in dry, tasteless hamburgers. Plenty of evidence surfaced that the composition of 'ground beef' included many substances other than beef. Unscrupulous purveyors, knowing their mischief would be undetectable, added non-beef ingredients such as organ meats and extenders such as flour and oatmeal and, if reports are to be believed, mixed in chopped dog, cat and rat meat. Borax and other chemicals were frequently added to preserve the ground beef and make it look good. Public prosecutions and reports of food-borne illness caused by eating hamburgers appeared regularly in newspapers and magazines. Hamburger sellers were frequently brought into court for poisoning their customers, and the hot sandwich acquired an unsavoury reputation.

Even after hamburgers had become an American institution in the 1920s, advocates for pure food frequently condemned them: Arthur Kallet and F. J. Schlink, authors of *100,000,000 Guinea Pigs, Dangers in Everyday Foods, Drugs, and Cosmetics* (1932), proclaimed that, 'The hamburger habit is just about as safe as walking in an orchard while the arsenic spray is being applied, and about as safe as getting your meat out of a garbage can standing in the hot sun. For, beyond all doubt the garbage can is where the chopped meat sold by most butchers belongs, as well as a large percentage of all the hamburger that goes into sandwiches.'

In addition, street vendors faced increasing obstacles. As automobiles began to clog the streets of America during the twentieth century, many cities passed laws licensing street vendors to prevent congestion. The result was that many vendors were required to move indoors, and new ways of feeding urban America developed – cafés, cafeterias, coffee shops, lunch counters, diners, roadside stands and eventually drive-ins – all of which would commonly serve hamburgers.

2

The Hamburger Chain

Hamburger sandwiches might have remained a lower-class food with a bad reputation had it not been for J. Walter ('Walt') Anderson, a short-order cook in Wichita, Kansas. In 1916 Anderson had saved enough money to purchase an old shoe-repair building and converted it into a hamburger stand. Like many other hamburger purveyors, he sold burgers for a nickel. To keep costs down, Anderson made thin, one-inch-square patties, which also permitted quick cooking. To overcome the negative perceptions of hamburgers, Anderson arranged for beef to be delivered twice a day, and sometimes more often, and he ground his own beef so that customers could watch him do so through glass windows. His approach was so successful that he opened three additional hamburger stands, all with carry out service. In 1920 the Wichita Eagle proclaimed Anderson 'King of the Hamburger'.

Walt Anderson wanted to expand his operation even further, but he lacked the capital to do so. Then he met Edgar Waldo ('Billy') Ingram, a Wichita estate agent and insurance man, who was flush with cash and looking for an investment. In 1921, the two created a partnership. From the beginning, Ingram believed that Anderson's model could be greatly

White Castle: the first White Castle hamburger stands were small by the standards of today's fast food outlets.

improved. Anderson and Ingram called their joint venture 'White Castle', and designed a new structure complete with turrets, imitating the Chicago Water Tower, which had been one of the few structures to survive the great Chicago fire of 1871. This was a symbol of permanence – quite different from the image of mobile hamburger stands that dotted the nation at the time. The dominant colour of the new design was white, which was intended to represent purity and cleanliness.

White Castle initially served only hamburgers, soft drinks, coffee and pie, but the menu expanded over the years. Employees were required to wear uniforms and observe high standards of cleanliness. Local butchers supplied the beef, which was ground at the outlet. When White Castle became larger, the company established its own meat-processing

Little girl enjoying a hamburger with a glass of milk during the 1930s.

plants, paper supplies and bun-baking operations to produce consistent products for all the outlets.

This new design was successful and, by 1924, White Castle had expanded to Omaha, Kansas City and St Louis. In 1925, the company served more than 84,000 hamburgers. Anderson sold his portion of the operation to Ingram, who continued to expand it, particularly in urban areas near bus and trolley stops and in locations close to large factories. As White Castle operated within wide geographical regions, the company could advertise over a wide area, thus increasing the sales in multiple outlets. White Castle placed ads in newspapers and on the radio, using the slogan 'Buy 'em by the sack'.

Ingram's business plan, which he called the 'White Castle System', had several components: efficiency and economy (nickel hamburgers, a limited menu and mass volume); standardization and simplification of the food-preparation process; prominent locations near mass-transit stops; a uniform and distinctive architecture; aggressive expansion of outlets; and a pleasant setting conducive to the consumer's enjoyment. To make sure this system was implemented properly, Ingram frequently visited many outlets. To save time travelling great distances, he acquired a used biplane that he flew to visit White Castle operations.

The White Castle System worked. By 1931, the company owned 131 outlets, far more than any other fast-food chain at the time. When the Depression hit, the company restructured its operation by closing unprofitable outlets and opening new ones in promising new areas. As White Castle burgers were still cheap, eating there was a small luxury that many Americans could afford. The company streamlined its operations by making and selling hamburgers at an increasing rate. It included discount coupons in its newspaper ads. The company also experimented with new products. One of these was milkshakes, but management decided that they took too long to make and the equipment was prone to breakdowns and difficult to fix. In addition, White Castle management believed that milkshakes ruined the customer's appetites for hamburgers, the company's flagship product, so the drinks were taken off the menu.

By 1935 White Castle was selling 40 million hamburgers

Walt Anderson and Edgar Waldo ('Billy') Ingram, founders of White Castle, used a biplane to visit their fast-food chain.

annually, which was a phenomenal success by any standard – especially during the deepest days of the Depression.

Clones and Competitors

White Castle's success spurred the development of other hamburger chains, often with similar-sounding names, such as White Mama diner in Worcester, Massachusetts, and the White Tavern Hamburger in Amsterdam, New York. The most successful clone was White Tower, launched by John E. Saxe, his son, Thomas E. Saxe, and an associate, Daniel J. O'Connell. After visiting White Castle, the partners opened their first restaurant near Marquette University in Milwaukee in 1926. Like White Castle, White Tower located its outlets at subway, trolley and bus stops frequented by workers going to and from factories. They specialized in five-cent hamburgers

White Mama: due to the incredible success of White Castle, knock-offs such as the White Mama diner in Worchester, Massachusetts, sprang up around the United States. They used similar names and products.

The White Tavern hamburger stand was a popular place in Amsterdam, New York, 1941.

almost identical to White Castle's, but also sold ham sandwiches, doughnuts, pies and beverages.

White Tower's outlets looked a lot like White Castle's, and White Tower's slogan, 'Take home a bagful', was an undisguised knock-off of White Castle's 'Buy 'em by the Sack'. Like White Castle, White Tower outlets were white to convey to customers the purity and cleanliness of the restaurants. Unlike White Castle, however, White Tower franchised their operation, requiring franchisees to construct a particular type of building and maintain a set menu. This was a formula for success and the chain expanded steadily throughout the Midwest. By the end of the 1920s White Tower was the largest hamburger chain in America. White Castle sued White Tower in 1929, the court ruling in favour of White Castle. White Tower was ordered to change its name and to remove all similarities to White Castle in its architecture and slogans. White Tower managed to maintain its name by paying White Castle a large sum of money, but it never fully recovered.

Other fast-food chains developed at the same time as White Castle and White Tower. In 1919 Roy Allen launched what became A&W Root Beer in Lodi, California. A&W franchised their operation, requiring franchisees to pay a small licensing fee, display the A&W logo and buy root beer syrup from the company. Other than these connections, little commonality existed among franchisees: they had no common architecture and no common menu, although most franchises sold hamburgers along with the root beer. Unlike White Castle, A&W franchises mainly focused on small towns rather than working-class neighbourhoods.

Another chain was Wimpy Grills, launched in 1934 by Edward Vale Gold in Bloomington, Indiana. The chain was named after the hamburger munching cartoon character, J. Wellington Wimpy, created in 1931 by Elzie Crisler Segar

White Tower also built upon the name, architectural design and merchandise of White Castle. In 1929 White Castle took White Tower to court, claiming trademark infringement, and won.

The interior of the White Tavern hamburger stand in Amsterdam, New York, 1941.

White Castle hamburger advert.

for his comic strip *Popeye the Sailor Man*. Wimpy was never able to afford a hamburger, so he tried to con others into buying one for him. His frequent plea, 'I'd gladly pay you Tuesday for a hamburger today', remains part of the American vocabulary. Wimpy Grills sold sandwiches and very large hamburgers (not by the sackful or bagful – one was enough). By 1939, the term 'wimpyburger' had become synonymous with a large hamburger.

Yet another hamburger chain was launched in 1936 by Bob Wian, who opened a ten stool diner called 'Bob's Pantry' in Glendale, California. It was successful and Wian enlarged

In *Popeye*, the 1980 movie, Paul Dooley played J. Wellington Wimpy.

J. Wellington Wimpy, created in 1931 by Elzie Crisler Segar for his comic strip *Popeye the Sailor Man*.

his establishment, turning it into a combination coffee shop and drive-in. At the time, White Castle's hamburgers were small, single-patty sandwiches. Wian bid for attention by splitting a sesame seed bun lengthwise into three slices and sandwiching two beef patties in between. He originally called his creation the 'fat boy', then changed it to 'Big Boy'. In 1937 Wian renamed his restaurant 'Bob's Big Boy'. Its icon was a plump youngster wearing red and white checked overalls with the words 'Big Boy' emblazoned across his chest. In his hand he carried a big triple decker hamburger. The company constructed 12-foot (3.7-metre) statues of the Big Boy and placed them in front of each restaurant in the chain. The flagship meal at Bob's was the 'Combo' – a Big Boy burger, fries and a small salad.

As Wian expanded his operation, the new units generally included coffee shops with interior seating as well as a drive in service. He also franchised his restaurant. The cost to set up a full-service Big Boy restaurant was $250,000, a princely sum in the 1940s and '50s. One unusual arrangement was that franchisees were free to substitute their own name for 'Bob's'. Hence, the Frisch Company opened Frisch's Big Boys throughout the Midwest, and 'Azar's Big Boy' could be found in Colorado. It was not an integrated operation, but a contractual relationship that funnelled Wian royalties (2 per cent on gross sales) in exchange for the use of the 'Big Boy' logo and the triple decker sandwich.

By the 1930s, virtually every medium sized city in America had drive-ins, roadside stands, diners and coffee shops – all of which served hamburgers. Hamburgers had evolved from a food fad into a standard menu item served across the country. Hamburger chains like White Castle, White Tower and A&W emerged throughout the country. R. B. Davenport's Krystal sold small square burgers in

Making hamburgers in a concession stand, National Rice Festival, Crowley, Louisiana, 1938.

Some hamburger stands were not much larger than a small room, such as the one in Dumas, Texas, 1939.

Chattanooga, Tennessee; there was the Royal Castle burger chain in Miami, the Toddle House chain in Cincinnati and the Snappy Service burger chain in Indiana. In California, Stan Burke opened Stan's Drive-In Coffee Shops in Bakersfield,

Stan's Drive-In, Los Angeles, California.

Fresno, Sacramento and Los Angeles. Along with many others, Burke claimed to have invented the cheeseburger.

World War II and the Post-war Period

During World War II, established hamburger chains faced serious problems due to labour shortages and the lack of meat, which was rationed during the war. Sugar was also rationed, and soda was in short supply. Hamburger chains sought new potential products to sell. One was the fried-egg sandwich. Eggs were fried in a metal ring and served on a hamburger bun, much like today's McDonald's Egg McMuffin. Potatoes became a more important menu item during the war. They were inexpensive, plentiful and not subject to rationing. Previously, French fries had been a

During the 1930s and '40s, hamburger stands were teenage hangouts. Hamburger Stand, Imperial County Fair, California, 1942.

minor offering in hamburger operations due to the difficulty of operating the equipment and safety issues related to working with boiling hot fat in the deep fryer. French fries, however, became popular during the war, and were fondly remembered afterwards.

French fries continued to be sold after the war, but as before were mainly discontinued because the deep-frying equipment with its boiling grease was dangerous for operators, who also found it difficult to tell when the fries were properly cooked. In the 1950s, technological improvements made possible safe, virtually foolproof fryers, and French fries returned to hamburger chains. Milkshake equipment also changed during the 1950s, and White Castle brought the beverages back to their menus. In 1958, White Castle test marketed a 'King Size' hamburger to compete with the increasing popularity of Bob's Big Boy, but their customers preferred the time-honoured 'slider'.

After the war, urban hamburger chains faced some new challenges. As the number of cars on US roads skyrocketed during the late 1940s and early 1950s, more Americans wanted to drive in for their burgers. Most inner city hamburger outlets did not have parking facilities, so could not benefit from this development. The greater availability of cars also made it possible for the middle classes to move out of the city and settle in suburbs, where there were no established hamburger chains. Crime, which increasingly affected inner cities after the war, was another problem for urban hamburger stands. Many stayed open 24 hours a day to serve workers, but this also made the outlets – and their customers – targets for late night crime. Many inner-city establishments became havens for the homeless, who used their dining areas to sleep in and the restrooms for washing, damaging the all-important 'clean' image that so many hamburger

On a date at the Hot Shoppe after the Woodrow Wilson High School regimental ball in Washington, DC, 1943. She ordered a hamburger and milk, while he got a hamburger and Coke.

White Castle hamburger stand interior.

chains tried to uphold. Finally, racial unrest hit the inner cities
and many whites fled to the suburbs. As a result of these
societal changes, the established inner city hamburger chains,
such as White Castle and White Tower, began to fade.

Many new chains were established in the post-war period.
For instance, Tommy's was launched in Los Angeles during
1946 by Tommy Koulax, who specialized in the chilli burger.
In 1948 Harry and Esther Snyder launched the In-N-Out
Burger in Baldwin Park, California. From its inception, it
was a drive-through operation complete with a two-way
speaker system. Unlike other fast-food purveyors, the Snyders
decided not to franchise their operation. This meant a much
slower growth pattern, and their second outlet didn't open
until 1951. Whataburger was founded in Corpus, Texas, in
1950. In 1953 Keith G. Cramer and Matthew Burns of
Jacksonville, Florida, opened a hamburger stand that would

evolve into Burger King. In San Diego, California, Robert O. Peterson started Jack in the Box in 1950. Dave Thomas opened his first Wendy's restaurant in 1962 in Columbus, Ohio. But by far the most important post-war hamburger chain was McDonald's.

3
The McDonald's Machine

American suburbs were largely a post-war phenomenon. Affluence and increasing car ownership made it possible for many middle-class families with young children to buy homes away from the inner cities, which were beset with problems. As suburban life flourished, new business models arose to serve the needs of families.

One model for feeding suburban families was developed by two brothers, Richard and Maurice McDonald. Born in New Hampshire, in 1930 they moved to Los Angeles, where they bought a small cinema. It was not much of a money-maker so, in 1937, to make ends meet, they opened an orange juice and hot-dog stand near the Santa Anita racetrack in Arcadia, a suburb of Los Angeles. Surprisingly, hot dogs and orange juice didn't sell, so they began offering barbecue and hamburgers. Still not satisfied with the stand's performance, in 1940 they moved to San Bernardino, a community about 100 miles east of Los Angeles, where they opened 'McDonald Brothers Burger Bar Drive-in'. They employed twenty female 'carhops' who took orders, delivered the food and collected payment from their customers. The brothers noticed that 80 per cent of their sales were hamburgers so they dropped the barbecue which, in any case, took too long to prepare. After

Hamburger stands during the 1930s were small with few stools, such as the one above in Alpine, Texas, 1939.

World War II they faced problems with employees. The economy was booming and many men who had been in the service were attending college on the GI bill. The small labour pool meant that the McDonald brothers ended up with drunken cooks and dishwashers, and carhops who seemed more interested in socializing than selling burgers.

The McDonald brothers were convinced that their target audience was families, so they tried to create an environment that would encourage suburbanites and discourage groups of teenagers, who did not buy much, and were likely to break or steal dishes, trays and flatware. Replaced by paper and plastic, breakable plates, glasses and cups became a thing of the past – as did the pretty girl carhops.

The brothers decided to tighten things up by reducing expenses and increasing profits through improved efficiency.

A central feature of their operation was an industrial assembly-line model popularized by Henry Ford, whose techniques had previously been adapted for use in food service in cafeterias, railway dining cars and at the Howard Johnson restaurant chain. The model included a division of labour into simple tasks that could be performed with a minimum of training. This meant that employees were essentially interchangeable and could easily be shifted from one task to another. This assembly-line system provided customers with fast, reliable and inexpensive food; in return, the McDonald brothers expected their customers to queue, pick up their own food, eat quickly, clean up their own rubbish and leave without delay, thereby making room for others.

To implement these ideas, the brothers redesigned the restaurant, installing larger grills and Multimixers. These were for making many milkshakes simultaneously in metal containers. After the milkshakes were made, the contents of the metal containers would be poured into paper cups. To speed up the process, the brothers reduced the length of the arm so that milkshakes could be made directly into the paper cups, thus eliminating a step. Eighty or more shakes were prepared in advance and held in a refrigerated case, thus speeding up the process of fulfilling orders.

This model created a militarized production system that was based on a workforce of teenage boys, who were responsible for simple, easily learned tasks: some heated the hamburgers, others packaged the food or poured the soft drinks and shakes and still others placed orders in paper bags. The new model did away with indoor seating, and streamlined the menu down to a few low-cost items in addition to fifteen-cent hamburgers and nineteen-cent cheeseburgers. The hamburger patties weighed only 1.5 ounces (45 grams) and all burgers came with the same condiments:

ketchup, chopped onion and two slices of pickles. The other items were ten-cent fries, twenty-cent shakes and large and small fizzy drinks. In the new 'self-service' restaurant, customers placed their orders at a window and ate in their cars. All food was served in disposable paper wrappers and paper cups, eliminating the problems of breakage and theft.

McDonald Brothers Burger Bar Drive-in was an octagonal building, which was not unusual in southern California at that time. When the renovated drive-in opened in 1948, it got off to a rocky start: customers honked their horns, expecting carhops to come out and take their orders. Eventually, customers got used to the new system and came back again and again for the low prices, fast service and good hamburgers. The McDonald brothers claimed that

The first McDonald's restaurant in San Bernardino, California, was in an octagonal-shaped building. It wasn't until 1954 that Richard J. McDonald and his brother Maurice developed the famous design of a glass-fronted building with 'golden' arches.

their employees could serve a customer who ordered a full meal – hamburger, fries and a beverage – in twenty seconds. Increased volume led to greater profits. By 1951, the brothers grossed $275,000, of which $100,000 was profit. Reports of their phenomenal success spread around the nation and in July 1952 *American Restaurant* magazine ran a cover story on the 'McDonald's New Self-Service System'. The brothers believed that they were ready to franchise their operation, so they began advertising.

As radical as their new design was, the McDonalds believed that they could make an even more efficient operation by changing the architectural layout; they also wanted a more distinctive design that would be easier to spot from the road, one that would make their drive-ins stand out from the hundreds of other fast-food establishments. Their new model restaurant was constructed with a forward-sloping glass front; the walls were painted in red and white stripes. Richard McDonald came up with the idea for the 'golden arches', which bisected the roof. Under the arches there was white tiling, implying cleanliness, and lots of glass, making the preparation of the food visible to all.

Even before the brothers completed construction on their new restaurant in San Bernardino, they began selling franchises based on the new design. Franchisees paid the McDonald brothers a relatively small fee and a percentage of their sales. Unlike previous food-service franchisers, the brothers demanded that every outlet be built exactly like their model, and that exactly the same food be prepared in exactly the same way. Their new model had no indoor dining; customers were expected to eat in their cars. A couple of inexpensive chairs and tables were provided outside for walk-up customers or for those who preferred not to eat in their vehicles. This model gave McDonald's a great advan-

The first McDonald's stands were small operations in comparison with today's large outlets.

tage over other emerging fast-food chains, for it promised consistency, predictability and safety. Many potential franchisees saw these requirements as limitations because they could not use existing buildings, and by the end of 1953 the brothers had sold only 21 franchises, of which just ten eventually became operating units. Two were in Phoenix, Arizona, and the rest were in the suburban Los Angeles area. Compared with other fast-food chains such as Dairy Queen, with its 2,600 outlets at the time, this was hardly a success.

The McDonald's restaurant in San Bernardino continued to attract large crowds. Many future fast-food entrepreneurs visited the San Bernardino site and were impressed with what they saw. In 1952, Matthew Burns and Keith G. Cramer visited McDonald's; the following year they opened the Insta-Burger King in Jacksonville, Florida, which later became Burger King. After a visit to McDonald's, restaurant owner Carl Karcher of Anaheim, California, decided to develop a fast-food chain of his own; he named it 'Carl's Jr'.

Glen Bell of San Bernardino studied the McDonald's operation and sought to develop something similar using Mexican food instead of hamburgers. He eventually launched the Taco Bell chain. James Collins, chairman of Collins Foods International, visited San Bernardino, took notes on the operation and opened up a Kentucky Fried Chicken franchise based on the brothers' design. Many other entrepreneurs opened McDonald's clones, and by 1954 many other fast-food operations were based on the model developed by the McDonald brothers.

Another visitor to McDonald's in San Bernardino was Ray Kroc, the owner of a Chicago company that manufactured Multimixers. Kroc had sold Multimixers to many fast-food franchisees, including Dairy Queen and Tastee-Freez. This experience gave Kroc a deeper understanding of the fast-food business and some knowledge of problems related to franchising. In the early 1950s, increased competition reduced the sales of Multimixers, and Kroc needed new outlets. He saw advertisements for McDonald's and was surprised to find that the McDonald brothers had purchased eight of his company's Multimixers. In 1954, he visited the McDonald brothers and was astounded by the crowds flooding the restaurant. Kroc saw the potential of the McDonald's operation. He met with the brothers and signed an agreement allowing him to sell McDonald's franchises nationwide. In the mid-1950s, franchising mainly involved assigning territories to franchisees for huge up-front fees. Kroc wanted to control McDonald's operations. He avoided territorial franchises by selling one store franchise at a time, thereby controlling the number of stores a licensee could operate. He also required strict conformity to operating standards, equipment used, menus, recipes, prices, trademarks and architectural designs. In 1955 Kroc created McDonald's

Ray Kroc, founder of McDonald's System, Inc.

System, Inc., and sold himself the first franchise in Des Plaines, Illinois, which opened in 1955. He intended it to be a model operation that would attract potential franchisees.

Meanwhile, Kroc hired Harry Sonneborn, who had worked for Tastee-Freez and had established its franchising operation. Sonneborn designed the McDonald's Franchise Realty Corporation, which purchased land in strategic locations and then rented it to McDonald's franchisees. In this way, McDonald's became one of America's largest landowners. The corporation made money off the rental agreement and if the franchisee violated the agreement, McDonald's could evict them. Franchisees then did basically whatever the

The first McDonald's in Des Moines, Iowa, 1955.

parent company wanted. In this way, Kroc controlled the franchise operations, ensuring uniformity, maintaining standards and generating profits.

By the end of 1959 there were more than 100 McDonald's operations. This early success rested partly on the managers selected to oversee operations. Kroc's mantra was 'Quality, Service, Cleanliness, and Value' which he tried to instil in every franchisee. Kroc also believed in training managers. He established Hamburger University, which offered a degree in Hamburgerology. The first class of fifteen students graduated in February 1961. Since then, tens of thousands of managers have taken the course.

Kroc had numerous disagreements with the McDonald brothers along the way. The brothers required Kroc to follow their architectural and operational design exactly but Kroc wanted to innovate. Kroc solved this problem by buying the brothers out for $2.7 million. The buyout included a provision that permitted the McDonald brothers to continue operating the original McDonald's outlet in San Bernardino and it offered some protection for the other existing franchisees.

There was no love lost between Ray Kroc and the McDonald brothers. Kroc built a new McDonald's restaurant across the street from the brothers' operation and tried to run them out of business. When the original McDonald's restaurant burned down, Kroc proclaimed his operation in Des Plaines the first real McDonald's hamburger outlet, and he later converted it into a museum. But this isn't actually the oldest surviving McDonald's restaurant. That honour goes to the McDonald's in Downey, California, which was one of the original outlets franchised by the McDonald brothers in 1953. It has been slightly modernized, and the proprietors have built a small museum celebrating the early years of the chain.

A significant component of the success of McDonald's was America's changing demographics. Earlier hamburger chains, such as White Tower and White Castle, were in urban areas. McDonald's targeted suburban America, which had grown rapidly after World War II. The suburbs were home to families with plenty of baby-boom children, and suburban life was dependent on the car. McDonald's tied franchising with fast food, cars and families, and did everything possible to prevent their outlets from becoming teenage hang-outs. Kroc expanded upon the policies established by the McDonald brothers by banning jukeboxes, vending machines and telephones. He refused to hire women until he was required to do so by law.

Within a decade of his first encounter with the McDonald brothers, Ray Kroc had revolutionized fast-food service. By 1963 McDonald's was selling one million burgers a day, and this was only the beginning. The company began

McDonald's success was in part based on its advertising, such as this bill-board, 1970s.

advertising nationally in 1966, the same year that it was first listed on the New York Stock Exchange. Kroc's model for success was emulated by virtually every new local, regional and national fast-food operation in America. McDonald's symbolized success and it generated huge profits. Ray Kroc had originally envisioned 1,000 outlets in the United States. When he died in 1984, at the age of 81, there were 7,500 McDonald's worldwide.

The McDonald's national promotional campaigns have been a significant reason for its success. Slogans such as 'You deserve a break today', which *Advertising Age* rated as the top advertising campaign of the twentieth century, and the chant, 'Two all beef patties, special sauce, lettuce, cheese, pickles, onions on a sesame seed bun', became national mantras. According to Eric Schlosser, author of

Fast Food Nation: The Dark Side of the All-American Meal
(2001), McDonald's spends more on advertising and promotion than any other brand.

In the 1950s, few American retailers targeted children with their advertising. The conventional wisdom was that children did not have money, which was true, so retailers targeted the adults who brought the children into stores. Kroc had aimed his promotions at middle-class suburban families. What he found was that children had 'pester power', and studies indicated that children often determined where their families ate. Children liked fast-food establishments, where it was easy for them to choose what they wanted to eat. Kroc set out to make visits to his outlets into 'fun experiences' for children. Ronald McDonald, an invention of a Washington, DC, franchisee, was selected as the company's national spokesperson in 1966.

The McDonald's outlet in Chula Vista, near San Diego, opened the first McDonaldland Park in 1972. Ten thousand people visited during its two-day grand opening. This proved to be such a success that McDonald's began opening brightly coloured Playlands, complete with playgrounds and mythical characters, at many of its outlets. The company has also linked much of its marketing with children's motion pictures. The McDonald's Happy Meal, inaugurated in 1979, packages a toy along with the food, and today McDonald's is the world's largest toy distributor. By 1980 the company had spent millions of dollars on child-orientated television advertising and local promotions, and the investment paid off: 96 per cent of American children recognized Ronald McDonald – second only to Santa Claus. McDonald's had uncovered a lucrative promotional axiom: brand loyalty begins with children, and advertising targeted at children today ensures such loyalty when they reach adulthood.

McDonald's frequently appeared in movies such as *Red Dawn*, 1984.

McDonald's also appeared in the film *Moscow on the Hudson*, starring Robin Williams, 1984.

Ray Kroc's success encouraged the growth of other fast-food chains, which readily adopted the McDonald's model. But when the competition introduced innovations, McDonald's needed to keep up. In 1967 Burger King launched a newly designed restaurant with indoor seating. This challenged one of the basic tenets of the McDonald's model: the customers eat in their cars. But by the 1960s, the novelty of eating in the car had worn off. It was also uncomfortable on hot and humid days and on cold winter days. Indoor eating areas permitted year-round climate control, and customers greatly appreciated the comfortable new Burger Kings. McDonald's countered with a new design featuring indoor seating, which was inaugurated in 1968. The design made it possible to challenge another of the basic McDonald's early tenets – that the chain would stay out of the cities – and since then, thousands of McDonald's franchises have successfully opened in urban areas.

Several chains, including Wendy's, Jack in the Box and Burger King, found that their customers liked to order at drive-through windows; McDonald's began installing drive-through windows in 1975. Today, take-out and drive-through sales account for about 60 per cent of fast-food income in America.

To keep up with or ahead of the competition, McDonald's regularly introduced new products, starting with a diversified menu in the 1960s. The Big Mac, with its two patties, originated with a Pittsburgh franchisee, who was trying to create something to compete with Burger King's 'Whopper'. It was released nationally in 1968. By 1977 McDonald's was serving a complete line of breakfast sandwiches and English muffins for busy workers and commuters to eat on the run. Other innovations include the Quarter Pounder, the McDLT and the McLean Deluxe, a 90 per cent fat-free hamburger, which never caught on.

Towards the end of the twentieth century, McDonald's, along with other large fast-food chains, faced new problems, many of them related to its workforce. Labour costs were rising, the employee turnover rate was high and reliable workers were hard to find. The economics of the fast-food business are based on low salaries, and McDonald's and other fast-food chains have intentionally engaged in anti-union activities to keep their payrolls down. In addition, companies have consistently lobbied against increased minimum wages and worker benefits. A related problem is the high turnover rate for workers, which at some outlets approached 300 per cent per year. This was partly caused by low pay, and also by the fact that part-time workers do not receive benefits, overtime or pay rises for long service. When McDonald's was growing quickly, during the 1950s and '60s, there was an almost inexhaustible supply of young workers who found few other opportunities for employment. As the baby-boom teens came of age, McDonald's was eager to hire them, considering teenagers more impressionable and more manageable than older workers. When the baby-boom bulge began to decline, McDonald's was obliged to seek non-traditional workers. The company began hiring women as a result of federal anti-discrimination laws and the need for good employees. Then it began hiring recent immigrants, the elderly and the disabled. This required more training and supervision, and McDonald's introduced more automation and touch-screen computerized cash registers that made counter duty easier.

Partly because of the company's enormous success, McDonald's has been criticized on a variety of fronts and it has occasionally responded positively to criticism. In the 1960s the company was criticized for the lack of African-

American managers in its restaurants, so McDonald's made an effort to recruit more black franchisees. When charged with promoting junk food, the company began selling salads, reduced the fat content of its hamburgers and changed the way its French fries were cooked. When charged with causing harm to the environment, specifically for its use of polystyrene foam in coffee cups and food containers, McDonald's responded by creating an alliance with the Environmental Defense Fund to make the company more environmentally friendly. They switched from polystyrene to paper products and encouraged recycling. The Environmental Defense Fund has estimated that since 1989 McDonald's has saved 150,000 tons of waste through the improved packaging that it has demanded of its suppliers. In addition, the company has purchased more than $4 billion worth of recycled materials for its own operations. As a result of its environmentally friendly programmes, McDonald's has received a good deal of positive press coverage.

McDonald's has also been criticized for its influence on its suppliers. The logic for this is simple: McDonald's is the largest purchaser of beef in the world and it has some responsibility for the practices of its suppliers. Criticism has focused on suppliers in developing countries, and particularly on the fact that rainforests in Brazil have been destroyed in order to clear land for cattle raising. The company changed its suppliers, specifically refusing to purchase beef from Brazil, and it has made substantial contributions to environmental groups. Further attacks have been made on McDonald's due to the working conditions at feedlots and slaughterhouses of the company's suppliers. Eric Schlosser maintains that, as a result of practices followed at McDonald's and other fast-food chains, meatpacking is the most dangerous job in the United States; he writes that practices followed by meatpackers 'facilitated the introduction of deadly pathogens, such as E. coli O157:H7, into America's hamburger meat'. When McDonald's finally required that ground beef be demonstrably safe, the company's suppliers acquired equipment that was used for better testing.

McDonald's has a massive influence on potato growers, and the company controls 7.5 per cent of the entire potato crop in the United States. Potential concern for genetically modified organisms encouraged McDonald's to state that it would no longer purchase genetically altered potatoes in the United States. In Europe McDonald's does not use genetically modified foods due to restrictions imposed by European Union and national laws.

McDonald's has also been charged with adversely affecting local cultures and businesses around the world. The company's success abroad has caused deep resentment in others who see McDonald's as a symbol for the United States, and who believe that its expansion threatens local culinary traditions. In France, José Bové demolished a McDonald's restaurant nearing completion, and similar actions have occurred in other European countries. McDonald's has pointed out that many of its foreign operations are locally owned, and most products used in McDonald's are produced locally.

McLibel

In 1986, the London branch of Greenpeace, the environmental activist group, targeted what it considered to be the evils of McDonald's. It distributed a six-page leaflet entitled 'What's Wrong with McDonald's? Everything You Don't Want to Know', which accused the company of promoting poverty, selling unhealthy food, exploiting workers and children, torturing animals and destroying the Amazon rainforest. It included statements accusing McDonald's of using 'lethal poisons to destroy vast areas of Central American rainforests'. Members of London's Greenpeace distributed the flyers for four years, often in front of McDonald's outlets. In 1989, McDonald's infiltrated Greenpeace by hiring detectives to determine who was responsible for the leaflet and its distribution. Based on this information, McDonald's issued writs against five members for distributing the leaflet, which the company claimed was libellous.

The United Kingdom libel laws require defendants to prove in court the truth of their statements. Previously, McDonald's had used British libel laws to silence its critics. During the 1980s, for instance, it threatened to sue British publications and organizations, prompting retractions and apologies from the press. The cost of losing a libel case, in both legal fees and damages, could be huge. Three Greenpeace activists appeared in court and apologized to McDonald's. The other two, Helen Steel and Dave Morris, decided to defend themselves. They were not given any legal help from the court, but they were assisted free of charge by the Haldane Society of Socialist Lawyers. This David-and-Goliath fight was dubbed 'McLibel'. As news of it spread, the British media seized upon it, and the trial often ended up as front-page news. Steel and Morris received help from a large numbers of volunteers, some of whom formed the McLibel Support Campaign to assist the defendants with research. The trial began in March 1994 and continued for three years, becoming the longest trial in British history.

It also was a public-relations disaster for McDonald's, which was required to defend itself regarding its labour, marketing, environmental, nutrition, food safety and animal-welfare practices. Steel and Morris forced the company's top executives to testify for days. During the testimony, it came out that McDonald's had spied on the defendants before and after the company had sued them, and that Scotland Yard had supplied information to McDonald's. The McSpotlight Website covered the trial and the alleged abuses by McDonald's worldwide. Email and press releases were sent out and 'Days of Action' were held around the world protesting against McDonald's policies. The original leaflet was translated into 27 different languages, and since 1990 an estimated three million copies have been handed out.

In the final judgement Morris and Steel were found to have libelled McDonald's and were fined £60,000. The judge claimed that most of the charges were unproven but he did find that McDonald's had exploited children, endangered the health of its customers, paid workers extremely low wages and opposed union activity. He also found that the company did bear responsibility for the cruelty inflicted upon animals by many of its suppliers.

Morris and Steel appealed against the decision and sued Scotland Yard. On 31 March 1999, the Court of Appeal overruled parts of the original McLibel verdict, supporting the leaflet's assertion that eating McDonald's food can cause heart disease and that workers were treated badly. It reduced the damages to £40,000. Steel and Morris refused to pay and appealed, directing the case to the British House of Lords, which refused to hear it. In 2000 Morris and Steel filed an appeal with the European Court of Human Rights, challenging the verdict and stating that the trial breached their right to a fair trial and their right to freedom of expression. In June 2004, the European Court of Human Rights declared their claim to be admissible. In February 2005, the court held that Steel's and Morris's rights of free expression had been violated, as they had not been given legal aid and therefore had been denied a fair trial.

McDonald's Today

Studying McDonald's is a hot academic topic, and many popular works have tried to dissect its success and examine the company's influence. Among the more famous studies are George Ritzer's *The McDonaldization of Society* (1993) which examines the social effects of McDonald's in the United States, and Benjamin Barber's *Jihad vs. McWorld* (1995) which uses McDonald's as a global symbol for modernization. Dozens of other works have examined the company's world-wide positive and negative impact.

The economic importance of McDonald's is recognized in the popular press. The *Economist* compares currencies using the price of a 'Big Mac' as the base for its index to make exchange rates understandable. It is based on the assumption that the Big Mac should cost the same no matter what country it is sold in. The differences in prices indicate under-valued or over-valued currencies.

The foreign affairs columnist Thomas Friedman used McDonald's as a measure of modernization – he proudly announced that no two nations with McDonald's ever went to war with each other. This was challenged in the 1990s when the United States and other NATO allies attacked Serbia, a nation that had had McDonald's operations before the war. During the war these establishments were vandalized by Serbians who viewed McDonald's as a symbol of the United States.

The Serbians were not the first to view McDonald's as an American symbol, and McDonald's has both benefited

Hamburgers appeared even in postcards, such as R. Crumb's 'Hamburger Hi-Jinx'.

and suffered as a consequence. McDonald's outlets have been trashed, bombed and boycotted due to the policies of the United States government. At other times and places, McDonald's has been considered a modernizing force that has improved the local diet.

By the end of the twentieth century, one out of every eight American workers had at some point been employed by McDonald's. Studies claim that 96 per cent of Americans have visited a McDonald's at least once. An estimated 22 million Americans eat at a McDonald's every day. The company is an icon of efficient and successful business and it is ingrained in popular culture throughout the world.

4
McDonald Clones

Burger King

In 1952, Matthew Burns of Long Beach, California, and his stepson, Keith G. Cramer, visited McDonald's in San Bernardino, California. Burns had invited Cramer, owner of Keith's Drive-In in Daytona Beach, Florida, to California to have a look at the McDonald's operation. Burns and Cramer liked what they saw and decided to create a similar hamburger restaurant in Florida. They also visited an inventor, George E. Read, in Santa Monica. Read had created two 'Miracle Insta Machines' for the fast-food trade: one made multiple milkshakes simultaneously, while the other, the 'Insta-Broiler', cooked twelve burgers in a wire basket so that both sides of the patty were exposed to flame simultaneously. Four hundred burgers could be turned out in an hour with one machine – a dream come true for a high-volume drive-in. The cooked patties slid from the basket into pans of sauce, ready to be placed on toasted buns. In 1953, using both machines, Cramer opened the Insta-Burger King in Jacksonville, Florida. His burgers sold for 18 cents, milkshakes were 18 cents, French fries 10 cents and soft drinks 10 cents.

Cramer and Burns franchised territorial rights to Insta-Burger to James McLamore and David R. Edgerton Jr, who opened several Insta-Burger-King outlets in Miami beginning in 1954. Despite the fact that Edgerton and McLamore both held degrees from Cornell University's School of Hotel Administration, they were unable to make a profit on these restaurants. Thinking they might have a better idea, they dispensed with the Insta-Broiler and created a flame broiler. They changed the name of their operation to Burger King and introduced the 'Whopper' hamburger – a quarter-pound beef patty on a sesame-seed bun with sliced onions, tomatoes, pickles and condiments. American cheese and bacon could be added for an additional expense. The basic Whopper was sold for 37 cents – a risky venture since, at that time, burgers were selling for 15 cents at McDonald's, their major competitor. The Whopper was an instant success and became the company's signature product. Their slogan, 'Burger King, Home of the Whopper', appeared in many of the company's advertisements. When the Jacksonville Insta-Burger King chain had financial troubles, Burns and Cramer were pushed out and eventually Edgerton and McLamore acquired the national rights to the system. They began a massive effort to franchise Burger King in 1961.

To improve skills among managers, McLamore and Edgerton opened Whopper College in 1963, two years after the McDonald's Hamburger University had been set up. They created a 'Burger King' character, attired in royal robes and wearing a crown, to appeal to children, and paper crowns have been used as a promotional device ever since. For its customers' comfort during insect season, Burger King began installing screens on its ordering areas and patios. These were subsequently replaced with glass, and air-conditioning was added later. Indoor eating areas became integral to Burger

King by 1967, a year before McDonald's created indoor dining. In some outlets Burger King experimented with drive-throughs along with a separate staff to run them. This proved too costly and was discontinued, only to be started up again some years later.

Burger King failed to regulate its franchises adequately and the franchisees felt free to diverge from the company standard. In 1964, Burger King created a consistent image for all its outlets. Standards for speed, cleanliness and quality were controlled by frequent, unscheduled visits by the company inspectors. Sales rebounded to such an extent that, in 1967, the company was acquired by Pillsbury. Pillsbury eliminated the little king logo, although it was later revived. Pillsbury also began a massive promotional campaign for Burger King using slogans and jingles such as 'Have it Your Way' and 'America Loves Burgers and We're America's Burger King'. In the 1980s Burger King launched an advertising blitz; McDonald's responded with their own massive advertising campaign. The result of the 'Battle of the Burgers', as it was dubbed, was that Burger King improved its market share vis-à-vis McDonald's.

As the company began to open franchises beyond the United States, it changed its name to Burger King International. Pillsbury was itself acquired in 1987 by the British multinational Grand Metropolitan, which merged with Guinness to become a company called Diageo. In 2002 Diageo sold Burger King to an equity sponsor group made up of Texas Pacific Group, Bain Capital and Goldman Sachs Capital Partners.

Jack in the Box

Robert O. Peterson founded Jack in the Box in San Diego in 1950. In 1951, Jack in the Box was sold to the San Diego Commissary Company (later called Foodmaker, Inc.). Initially Jack in the Box served a simple menu of hamburgers, French fries and milkshakes. Although the company experimented with other products such as tacos and sandwiches, the hamburger has remained its centrepiece.

Jack in the Box franchises were sold mainly in southern California. The distinctive feature of its architecture was a two-storey-high sign topped with the familiar clown face of the classic children's toy. Jack in the Box was one of the first fast-food chains to systematically incorporate drive-through windows in its outlets. In 1968, Foodmaker, Inc., became a wholly owned subsidiary of Ralston Purina. At the time, Jack in the Box maintained 870 units. In the 1970s the company began serving breakfast. The 'Breakfast Jack' and the Eggs Benedict sandwich were introduced in 1971, and other breakfast foods such as omelettes were introduced in 1976.

In 1975 ads for Jack in the Box ended with the phrase 'Watch out, McDonald's!' By 1979, the company had expanded to 1,100 units, but it soon reorganized itself by dropping some of those outlets and diversifying the menu. Jack in the Box was the first fast-food chain to serve salads. In a leveraged buyout an investment group acquired Foodmaker, Inc., from Ralston Purina in 1985. Foodmaker, Inc., changed its name to Jack in the Box, Inc., in 1999. In 2005 Jack in the Box was the fifth largest hamburger chain in America, with 1,670 outlets nationwide.

Carl's Jr.

Like many others, restaurateur Carl Karcher of Anaheim, California, visited McDonald's and was inspired to develop a fast-food hamburger chain of his own. In 1956 he opened a mini version of his existing restaurant, called Carl's, and named the new establishment 'Carl's Jr.' Karcher soon opened another in nearby La Brea, and within ten years the company had 24 outlets in southern California.

The company incorporated as Carl Karcher Enterprises, Inc. (CKE), in 1966. Two years later the company began an expansion plan with an enlarged version of the Carl's Jr. restaurant, complete with larger dining rooms, attractive architecture and piped-in music. The main menu items were hamburgers, hot dogs, fries, and malts. By 1975, the company had about 100 outlets in California; in 1981, CKE went public. CKE sold Carl's Jr. franchises nationwide. The corporation co-branded with Texaco and many Carl's Jr. outlets are now inside Texaco petrol stations. By 2004, CKE had more than 3,400 outlets.

Wendy's

Dave Thomas worked for Kentucky Fried Chicken and Arthur Treacher's Fish and Chips before he opened his first Wendy's restaurant in 1969 in Columbus, Ohio. Thomas believed that Americans wanted larger hamburgers than those offered by other chains; probably inspired by White Castle's little square burgers, he opted for a square, quarter-pound beef patty – burgers could be ordered with two and, later, three patties. Along with the patties were multiple strips of bacon and cheese. He charged 55 cents for the basic

Dave Thomas, founder of Wendy's hamburger fast-food chain.

large sandwich, which was a risk, as McDonald's was charging only 18 cents for their hamburgers at the time. With the available patties, bacon, cheese, sliced vegetables and condiments, the Wendy's 'Old Fashioned' hamburger could be ordered 256 different ways, the company claimed. For his market, Thomas concentrated on young adults, as opposed to the children targeted by other chains. He correctly judged the willingness of young adults to purchase an expensive hamburger.

Beginning in 1970, Dave Thomas began expanding his operation into other Ohio cities. In 1972 the first out-of-state

Wendy's was opened in Indianapolis. Wendy's went from having nine outlets in 1972 to 1,818 six years later, and the company went public in 1975. One reason for Wendy's early success was its drive-through windows, which were installed in 1971. Drive-through sales meant that less space was needed for parking facilities or indoor tables. McDonald's and Burger King followed Wendy's example.

In addition to hamburgers and French fries, Wendy's diversified its menu to include chicken sandwiches, the Frosty (similar to the milkshake), baked potatoes and chilli. The salad bar was added in 1979. In September 1986, Wendy's introduced the Big Classic, a quarter-pound hamburger on a bun resembling a Kaiser roll.

Wendy's, like other fast-food chains, has advertised extensively on television. In 1984 the company launched the famous 'Where's the Beef?' commercial. Later that year, the slogan became a catchphrase of the Walter Mondale campaign when Mondale ran against President Ronald Reagan. Dave Thomas appeared in Wendy's advertisements beginning in 1989. Today, Wendy's is the third largest US hamburger chain, with more than 6,600 outlets in the United States and 34 other countries.

In-N-Out Burger

In 1948 Harry and Esther Snyder launched their first In-N-Out Burger in Baldwin Park, California. It offered a simple menu of hamburgers, cheeseburgers, French fries, soft drinks and milkshakes. From its inception it was a drive-through operation complete with a two-way speaker system. Unlike other fast-food chains, the Snyders decided not to franchise their operation. This meant a slower growth pattern, and they didn't open a second outlet until 1951. By the time Harry Snyder died, in 1976, there were still only eighteen In-N-Out Burger outlets. But the chain has remained in family hands and it has continued to prosper.

To train managers for its outlets, the company established In-N-Out University. The company pays its employees significantly more than mandated minimum wages, and it offers workers a benefits package that includes dental, medical, vision and life insurance. As a result, In-N-Out enjoys lower employee turnover than other fast-food chains.

While the official menu has changed little since its inception, a 'Secret Menu' exists. This consists of special items and variations on the regular menu selections, all of which are listed on the company's website. These include the '2x4' – two meat patties layered with four slices of cheese – 'Animal Style', where the burger is fried in mustard and served on a bun with the usual condiments, and 'Protein Style', where the meat is wrapped in lettuce, not a bun. Shakes can be made in combination flavours, as can fizzy drinks.

In-N-Out Burger maintains its own meat-packing facility which dispatches ground beef to its outlets several times a week. Outlets have no microwaves or freezers. Fresh potatoes are peeled every day for the French fries. The shakes are made from ice cream, with no artificial thickeners. The family has declined offers to sell the chain, which today has its headquarters in Irvine, California. There are 150 outlets in California, Nevada and Arizona, many of which now have indoor seating. In 2004, the original In-N-Out Burger location was closed, and fans of the chain hope to see it turned into an In-N-Out Museum.

Bob's Big Boy originated in Glendale, California. Its double-patty burger gained popularity during the 1940s and '50s. Today, Big Boy Restaurants International is launching a new architectural design.

The interior of the new Big Boy restaurants models the restaurants of the 1950s.

Retro Burgers

Pre-World War II hamburger chains have survived into the twenty-first century. Bob's Big Boy in Burbank, California, remains a hot spot, particularly on Friday nights when restored vintage cars assemble in the restaurant's parking lot. Meanwhile, Big Boy Restaurants International, now headquartered in Warren, Michigan, has more than 400 outlets in the United States and Japan. The Krystal Company, headquartered in Chattanooga, Tennessee, continues to offer its small square burger. Since 2004 the company has sponsored a hamburger eating contest and, in 2007, the winner consumed 103 hamburgers in eight minutes, taking home $10,000 prize money.

Nostalgia for the golden age of the hamburger drive-in – the 1950s – has served as a springboard for new chains attempting to recreate the atmosphere of that era. Sonic, for instance, which began in Shawnee, Oklahoma, is the only national food chain that has retained carhops as an integral part of its operation. Today there are almost 3,000 Sonic Drive Ins across the United States. Fuddrucker's, a casual dining restaurant, claims to serve the 'world's greatest hamburger'. The all-beef patty weighs up to one pound (450 grams), and the restaurants provide a self-service bar so that customers can add their own condiments. Fuddrucker's originated in San Antonio, Texas, in 1980. Today the company operates more than 200 restaurants in 30 states. Johnny Rockets, launched in Hollywood in 1986, offers hamburgers and shakes, table-top jukeboxes and chrome-heavy 1950s decor. Yet another retro chain, Fatburger, was launched in Los Angeles in 1952, but it did not begin to franchise outlets until 1980. Their 'Kingburger' is made from 'fresh never frozen lean beef' and served to the accompaniment of 1950s hits on the jukebox.

Hamburger stands advertised in various ways. One common way of advertising in the 1930s was through matchbook covers. The above advertises The Night Hawk restaurants, featuring the 'Frisco Burger'. Once a large chain, a single Night Hawk restaurant survives today in Austin, Texas.

Yet another famous hamburger stand was Subway Hamburgers in Schreveport, Louisiana. It features home and office delivery via motorcycle.

Since the 1920s, thousands of smaller hamburger establishments – some with a single restaurant – have been common throughout America. To gain visibility and distinguish themselves from their competition, these restaurants produced a great variety of hamburgers with unusual names: Frisco Burgers were produced by Night Hawk restaurants in Austin, Texas; Subway Hamburgers in Schreveport, Louisiana; Battle Burgers in Greensboro, North Carolina; Glorified Burger in Lincoln, Nebraska; Kabab Burgers in Hollywood, California; Oceanburgers in Rolla, Missouri; Swiss Burgers in New York City; Big Tex Burgers in Bloomington, Indiana; and Biff Burgers in Okeechobee, Florida.

Hamburger stands used unusual names for their specials, such as the
'Glorified Hamburgers' in Lincoln, Nebraska, 1938.

5

The Hamburger Experience

By strict definition, the true hamburger is a cooked ground beef patty served in a bun. Back in the days of its origins, the beef was often mixed with suet to make it juicier, and sometimes chopped onions, onion juice or garlic were added for flavour. Over the years, myriad variations have been introduced, and the size, shape, composition and flavour of the hamburger have been subject to change.

Some hamburger recipes call for eggs (to keep the beef moist and prevent the patty from crumbling) or for starchy extenders such as bread soaked in milk, breadcrumbs, cornflakes or oatmeal. Some people prefer a blend of ground meat, adding lamb, veal or pork to the beef. And over the years unscrupulous vendors may have added any number of unsavoury fillers and adulterants to their hamburger patties. The patty can be cooked in various ways, grilling and frying being the most common. The frying medium may be the rendered fat from the beef itself, or oil, shortening or butter. Hamburger patties are often fried with onions and served with gravy.

Hamburger sandwiches were initially made with thinly sliced bread. But as burgers got bigger and juicier, more substantial bread was required. Hot food served in a bun wasn't a new idea: hot dogs had been sold this way by American street vendors at least since the 1870s, and hot dog buns had been manufactured by that time. But it wasn't until the late nineteenth century that buns were produced especially for hamburgers. Today, most hamburgers are served on soft white buns, often topped with sesame seeds, but you can also get hamburgers served on an English muffin, 'Taco burgers' enfolded in tortillas, and 'Greekburgers' tucked into pitta bread.

Condiments add a creative flourish to the presentation of a hamburger sandwich. Hamburg steak and other chopped-meat dishes were often accompanied by certain sauces, seasonings or garnishes even before the hamburger first met the bun. Salt, pepper, mustard and ketchup, for instance, were commonly added to these earlier dishes. Other recommended condiments in the early days were Worcestershire sauce, horseradish, nutmeg, lemon juice and sliced gherkins. Mayonnaise became an option when its commercial production began in the early twentieth century. Prior to the 1930s there's no record of tomatoes and lettuce being included in a hamburger sandwich. After World War II, a variety of other condiments were added, including ranch dressing, salsa, soy sauce, barbecue sauces and a host of 'secret sauces'.

As soon as the popularity of the standard hamburger had been established, variations began to emerge. By the 1920s, a slice of cheese was placed on the patty to make a cheeseburger. American cheese was the original choice, but later blue cheese, Swiss, Cheddar and other cheeses were used to make cheeseburgers. Strips of bacon were added to make a bacon burger. Chilli sauce transformed the sandwich into a chilli burger. Pizza sauce and mozzarella cheese would help create a pizzaburger. Hundreds of other combinations have been conceived using items like squashed beans,

Outside a MOS Burger stand at Nara, Japan.

mushrooms, carrots, eggs, guacamole, olives, chilli peppers and sauerkraut. For the calorie-conscious there have been 'lo-cal' burgers, made with very lean beef, and low-fat burgers in which part of the beef is replaced with soy products and other such non-meat fillers. Those willing to pay the hefty price can enjoy hamburgers made from Kobe beef, from beer-fed and hand-massaged cows renowned for the flavour and marbled texture of their meat. Kobe beef initially came from cattle raised in Japan, but now they are also raised in New Zealand and the United States. Today, some commercial outlets serve hamburgers that have been prepared outside the United States; the cooked patties are frozen and then shipped to the outlets where they are heated (often in a microwave oven) just before serving.

Burger Diversity

These days hamburgers are sometimes made from turkey, chicken, clams, rabbit, fish, pork or lamb; there are also meatless burgers ('veggie burgers') that get their substance and texture from soy protein, starchy vegetables, fruit slices, beans or nuts. The Hula Burger, for instance, complete with sliced pineapple, cheese and no meat on a bun, was developed in Cincinnati for Catholics to eat on Fridays and during Lent. The Boca Burger, created by Max Shondor, was introduced in 1993. These soy-based burgers have become a mainstay of vegetarian meals in the US, and non-vegetarians are taking to them as well.

You Want Fries with That?

Side dishes for the hamburger have varied over the years. French fried potatoes were the recommended accompaniment for Hamburg Steak, so they naturally became the standard side dish for a hamburger sandwich. During the nineteenth century in the United States, potatoes were usually fried in lard. By the 1870s, fried potatoes were standardized into particular shapes and sizes: in America, paper-thin rounds of potato, fried until shatteringly crisp, were called Saratoga chips, or potato chips; thicker sticks of potato, which remained soft on the inside, became 'French fried potatoes', which was shortened to 'French fries' by 1918. In Britain, a different terminology developed: long rectangular strips of potato became 'chips', and thin, crisp-fried potato slices were 'crisps'.

By the early twentieth century, French fries were occasionally found on café and diner menus. Easily eaten with the fingers, at their best when fresh and hot, they would become a perfect fit for the fast-food culture. But French fries didn't catch on right away; it's surprisingly hard to make them well, and the process requires time and attention. Huge numbers of potatoes have to be peeled and cut several times a day, according to demand. A big pot of fat – lard, shortening, or oil – has to be kept at a constant temperature of 340–70°F (170–90°C), ready for the next batch of potatoes. Just having that boiling fat on the stove is a hazard to everyone in the kitchen. The frying must be carefully timed and the fries served right away before they turn limp and soggy. Cooks needed special training to get all this right and, even then, accidents involving hot oil convinced many hamburger-stand operators and managers that French fries just weren't worth the trouble.

During World War II, when meat was rationed, hamburger-stand operators had to find alternatives for the scarce beef hamburger. Potatoes were not rationed, and they were abundant and cheap, so during the war French fries became a staple on restaurant menus. Even after the war, when rationing ended, the demand for French fries increased. The combination of hamburgers and French fries was just another version of the 'meat and potatoes' combination that has been at the core of the American diet since the eighteenth century. Still, some hamburger chains, such as White Castle, stopped making French fries before World War II because of the hot-oil hazard. In the 1950s, with the invention of new, safer commercial fryers, it became much easier to turn out perfectly cooked French fries; by the 1970s, fryers included automatic timers and lifts that produced superior French fries with little risk to the kitchen staff.

In the United States, French fries are usually salted and then dipped in ketchup. In some European countries, notably

Belgium and the Netherlands, mayonnaise is the sauce of choice, and Indonesian-style peanut sauce is also popular. In Great Britain chips are often sprinkled with malt vinegar.

French fries became the flagship product at McDonald's. The founders of the chain, Richard and Maurice McDonald, believed that their French fries were one of the important reasons for their success. They perfected the way fries were made and promoted the relationship between hamburgers and fries. The brothers used fresh Russet Burbank potatoes, which were peeled and thinly sliced. Cooked in special fryers, the fries emerged with a crisp texture on the outside and a soft cooked texture on the inside that became the hallmark of McDonald's fries. As the chain began to grow in the 1960s, dozens of different potato suppliers were contracted, and the reliable uniformity of McDonald's French fries declined. In addition, fresh Russet potatoes were available only seven months of the year. Ray Kroc, who acquired McDonald's from the McDonald brothers, began looking for better ways to prepare and distribute their French fries.

French fries had been commercially frozen since 1946, but the problem was that the potato flavour disappeared when they were fried. Idaho potato grower J. R. Simplot started producing frozen French fries in 1953, but sales were disappointing. Housewives didn't seem to want to deep-fry the frozen potatoes, so Simplot looked for fast-food chains that might be interested in the labour-saving benefits of his frozen fries. Simplot met Ray Kroc in 1965 and the world of the French fry has never been the same since. Working with the Simplot potato company, McDonald's researchers solved the problems – they sliced the potatoes, quick-fried them at 300°F (150°C) to remove moisture and froze them. McDonald's found that the fries tasted best when cooked in a mixture of 93 per cent beef tallow and 7 per cent soy oil. By 1972, virtually all McDonald's French fries were prepared in this way. Other chains emulated this process.

McDonald's was still frying potatoes in some beef fat in 1989, when vegetarians complained that the company had not informed customers that the fries were prepared using an animal product. In addition, nutritionists began to criticize the amount of cholesterol in the fries. In 1990, with considerable fanfare, McDonald's announced that they had switched to vegetable oil with 'added natural flavourings'. When it was disclosed that 'flavourings' included small amounts of beef tallow, vegetarians struck back: outraged Hindu customers in Bombay ransacked a McDonald's restaurant. The company denied that any beef product had ever been used in its restaurants in India. In the United States, a small group of vegetarians sued McDonald's for falsely claiming that the fries were vegetarian, a claim that the company denied making. McDonald's eventually settled out of court, agreeing to post an apology on the company's website and to pay $10 million to vegetarian organizations and to the twelve individuals involved in the suit.

Potatoes are the number-one vegetable in the American diet, and a large proportion of potatoes eaten are fried. Approximately one-quarter of all vegetables consumed by children are potato chips and French fries, and this increases to about one-third in the teenage years. Nutritionists have objected to the amount of cholesterol (if fried in beef fat), total fat, saturated fat, trans fats and sodium in fast-food fries, and obviously these dietary drawbacks have a great effect on children and teenagers because they eat a lot of fries.

During the past 50 years, the serving size of fast-food fries has steadily increased. Initially, McDonald's only offered a 'large' 2-ounce (57-gram) size. Today, a 'small' order of McDonald's fries is 2 ounces, and for years a 'large' weighed in at 6 ounces (170 grams). Then McDonald's 'supersized' that to 8 ounces (227 grams). Due to public pressure that resulted from Morgan Spurlock's documentary film, *Super Size Me*, and his subsequent book, *Don't Eat this Book*, McDonald's discontinued this size, but other fast-food chains continue to serve 8-ounce portions of fries.

McDonald's has continued to innovate in the way its French fries are prepared. It was the first fast-food company to employ computers to adjust cooking times and temperatures automatically. It created a rapid-frying system for frozen potatoes that pared down the delivery time by 30 to 40 seconds. When you have millions of customers ordering fries, even this seemingly small amount of time makes a big difference: the time saved easily covers the cost of the equipment.

Eric Schlosser, author of *Fast-Food Nation*, has written that the special taste of McDonald's French fries does not come from the type of potatoes, frying technology or equipment used to prepare them; other chains buy from the same sources and use similar equipment. What gives today's McDonald's fries their unique taste is the chemical flavourings added to the oil.

Annual sales of frozen French fries have grown dramatically over the past 50 years, and today French fries are the single most popular fast food in America. In 1970 sales of frozen French fries surpassed those of fresh potatoes in the United States. By 2000 annual sales of frozen French fries worldwide had grown to more than $1.9 billion.

An exception to the trend towards frozen fries is In-N-Out Burger, where the French fries are still made fresh, from scratch. Depending on the season, the company uses

Kennebec or Russet potatoes. Each potato is peeled and cut by hand shortly before frying in cottonseed oil. In-N-Out Burger's 'secret menu' offers a variety of different types of fries: 'Cheese Fries' are drizzled with melted cheese; 'Animal Fries' are topped with cheese and grilled onions; and 'Fries Well-Done' are fried for longer than usual, making them crisper.

As fast-food chains moved abroad, so did production of frozen French fries. Russet Burbank potatoes, which originated in the United States, are grown in many countries today expressly for making French fries. As of 2004, the United States remains the world's largest producer of frozen French fries; The Netherlands ranks second and Canada third. French fries have also become entangled in international politics. When France refused to join the American-led coalition against Iraq in 2003, some Congressional Republicans urged that the name 'French fries' be changed to 'liberty fries' or 'freedom fries'. A few die-hard Republican restaurant owners may have changed the wording on their menus, but the idea never really caught on.

Another common side dish for burgers is batter-coated, deep-fried onion rings. Advocates claim that onion rings were invented by the Pig Stand restaurant chain in the 1920s. No primary source evidence has been found to support this claim, and recipes for battered, deep-fried vegetables, including onions, were present in American cookbooks well before the twentieth century. In 1955, frozen breaded onion rings were manufactured by Sam Quigley in Nebraska. By 1959 he was engaged in a profitable business, selling operation 'Sam's Onions'. Other companies began manufacturing them for home use and for fast-food outlets. Onion rings did not become a popular fast food until the 1970s. In 1973 Dairy Queen began serving them, followed by Jack in the

Box in 1979. Today, Burger King also serves onion rings, as do A&W Root Beer, Carl's, Jr., Sonic and many others.

Washing it Down

Late nineteenth-century lunch wagons served coffee with hamburgers. When bottled soft drinks became popular at the beginning of the twentieth century, hamburger vendors offered colas, root beers and carbonated fruit-flavoured beverages. From its inception, White Castle sold fizzy drinks. Virtually all fast-food chains have sold soft drinks ever since. As the cost of production is low and the ingredients – water, carbon dioxide, sweeteners, colourings and flavourings – are cheap, carbonated drinks are high-profit items for fast-food operations.

Milkshakes have also been part of the hamburger history. They first became popular at drugstore lunch counters and soda fountains in the late nineteenth century. As an electrical appliance was required, milkshakes didn't appear at hamburger stands until the vendors moved indoors. With the invention of practical electric blenders by Hamilton-Beach in 1911, milkshakes and similar drinks, such as malts, became popular, particularly during Prohibition, when stronger drinks were not an option. Fast-food restaurants began selling milkshakes by the 1930s.

In the late 1930s, the invention of the Multimixer permitted several milkshakes to be made simultaneously. Salesman Ray Kroc was so impressed with the invention that he purchased the rights to the Multimixer in 1939. After World War II Kroc sold them to ice-cream chains such as Tastee Freez and Dairy Queen. In the early 1950s, Richard and Maurice McDonald had purchased eight Multimixers, which made it possible to sell 20,000 shakes a month. Kroc was impressed with this number, and also with the hundreds of customers he saw queuing to buy hamburgers, fries and shakes.

Since the 1950s, milkshakes have been an integral part of most fast-food operations. In some places they're still made from fresh milk, ice cream and syrups, but many chains make their shakes out of pre-fabricated mix with a flavouring syrup and milk. The ice-cream-based chains have developed all sorts of frozen dairy drinks, like Dairy Queen's Blizzard (which has sweets or biscuits (cookies) blended in).

By the mid-twentieth century, the traditional American hamburger sandwich and its accompaniments had largely been settled. As fast-food chains moved outside the United States, their elements changed to suit the culinary traditions of other nations and peoples.

6

The Global Burger

While the hamburger sandwich originated in the United States, similar foods had developed in the United Kingdom. Beef was highly prized in England, and Hamburg beef was considered the best. Before the advent of refrigeration, it was impossible to send fresh beef from Germany to England, so the beef was salted and spiced, shipped to England by boat and sold at a premium. From the leftover scraps, sausages were made. The 1758 edition of Hannah Glasse's *The Art of Cookery* included a recipe for making Hamburg-style sausages, using English beef of course (see p. 125). The recipe even suggested that the sausage be eaten with bread, foreshadowing the hamburger sandwich.

The first recipe entitled 'Hamburg Sandwiches' – slices of cold Hamburg sausages between two slices of bread with condiments – was published in Charles Hermann Senn's *Récherché Side Dishes* (1901) (see p. 127). As Hamburg sausage was sold at Fortnum & Mason's in London, it was an expensive upper-middle-class sandwich, as opposed to the cheap working-class hamburger sandwich that had emerged in the United States.

The American version of the hamburger sandwich arrived in Europe with the American military during World

War I. It was an ideal food for a military force – quick and easy to make, fresh and hot, easy to eat and requiring no plates or utensils. As hamburgers were made with scrap beef and whatever bread that was available, they were cheap but relatively nutritious and filling. And at this time, when hamburgers had become common fare in the United States, they were a welcome 'comfort food' for the American soldiers overseas.

The first evidence for commercial hamburger sandwiches served outside the United States appeared in Paris, where Jack Baker opened a restaurant catering to American expats and tourists during the 1920s. Baker served several 'American' foods, including hamburgers, but sales were limited and hamburgers did not catch on in France at that time. Hamburgers were served in French restaurants after World War II. These often had unusual names, such as Hamburger Americaine and Hamburger Provençal, and were often served to visiting American tourists.

During and after World War II, the American military served hamburgers at its military installations in western Europe, northern Africa and throughout the Pacific; local entrepreneurs served hamburgers as a way of attracting Americans to their establishments. Even though hamburgers were not commonly served outside the United States until decades after World War II, many non-Americans were first exposed to them through the American military. It was these connections than provided the base for the globalization of the hamburger during the 1970s and 1980s.

The burger's attraction for people in other countries was similar to that in America: it was inexpensive, convenient, versatile, filling and, in many circles, even trendy. Chains provided a reassuring uniformity: when travellers visited new cities, hamburger chain restaurants offered something familiar. Hamburger establishments caught on quickly in other parts of the world, and today there are few countries that do not sport an American fast-food restaurant.

English-speaking Hamburgers

Canada

Canada was the hamburger's first testing ground outside the United States. Canada's 3,145-mile-long border with the United States and a common language have encouraged culinary interactions for hundreds of years. Hamburgers followed a similar path in Canada as they did in the United States. They were served in Canadian restaurants by the early twentieth century, and American fast-food chains, such as White Castle, opened outlets in Canada before World War II. After the war, virtually all American hamburger chains launched operations in Canada, and their success encouraged the chains to open outlets in other countries. McDonald's, for instance, opened its first non-American operation in Canada in 1967 and, based on this experience, shortly thereafter set up shop in Australia, the United Kingdom and Europe. Burger King followed a similar trajectory. It opened its first outlet in Canada in 1969 and its first outlet in Australia two years later. Burger King commenced operations in the United Kingdom during the 1970s.

Australia and New Zealand

Burger King opened its first overseas outlet in a suburb of Perth, Australia, in 1971. At the time, another restaurateur had already trademarked the name 'Burger King'. The Australian franchisee, John Corwin, selected the name 'Hungry Jack's' to be used for subsequent Burger King outlets in Australia. Hungry Jack's served a Burger King menu with such additions as the 'Aussie Burger', which contained egg, bacon and cheese but no beef. When the Australian trademark for the name 'Burger King' lapsed, the company acquired it and wanted to rename all its Australian outlets. Corwin objected, refusing to change the names of his franchises. Beginning in 1996, the company opened restaurants in Australia and New Zealand under the name 'Burger King'; these often ran into competition with nearby Hungry Jack's outlets. Corwin sued Burger King and won, and was paid $75 million in damages by Burger King for breach of his franchise agreement. In 2002, Burger King exited the Australian market. Today Hungry Jack's Pty Ltd is a privately owned hamburger chain which also operates outlets in New Zealand.

Other hamburger chains have developed in Australia, although none are as large as McDonald's, Burger King and Hungry Jack's. In addition to Aussie Burgers, Australian hamburger restaurants offer optional items such as beetroot, eggs, bacon and pineapple. Other specialities often include a burger made with a mixture of beef and lamb.

Like Australia, New Zealand came to know the hamburger through the American military during World War II. In addition to McDonald's, Burger King and Hungry Jack's, indigenous chains have sprung up, including Burger Fuel, which sells gourmet burgers (beef, chicken, fish and chickpea) as well as the usual fast-food accompaniments. Fergburger, founded in 2001, specializes in gourmet hamburgers. In addition to the typical hamburger, Fergburger offers chicken burgers, breakfast burgers, lamb burgers, cod burgers, falafel burgers, venison burgers and other exotic fare. They also have breakfast burgers. Their 'Big Al' features two patties of prime New Zealand beef, two eggs, several slices of bacon, cheese and beetroot, as well as the usual lettuce, tomatoes, onions and other condiments. The Kiwi burger is served in many New Zealand restaurants. It is based on the Kiwi salad – lettuce, ham, boiled eggs and beets. In the McDonald's Kiwi Burger, the ham is replaced by the beef patty.

United Kingdom

McDonald's was not the first American hamburger chain in the United Kingdom. That honour goes to the Wimpy Grill. In 1953 its founder, Eddie Gold, offered the UK rights to Joseph Lyons and Co. of London, who had operated a chain of tea rooms called 'Lyons Corner Houses' since 1894. On a trial basis, Lyons opened a Wimpy counter in its Coventry Street Corner House in London. It was perfect timing on Lyons's part. The American military had introduced hamburger culture into Britain during World War II. By the early 1950s, beef rationing had ended and the British public was open to a new, inexpensive food from America. When Lyons offered Wimpy burgers at the Ideal Home Exhibition in 1954, they sold an average of 10,000 burgers a week. Lyons finalized the arrangement with Gold and began opening Wimpy restaurants. Unlike the fast-food chains that were developing in the United States, Wimpy served their burgers on a plate, with cutlery, and orders were delivered to the table by waiters. In 1957, Lyons created a subsidiary company, Pleasure Foods Ltd, to franchise Wimpy Bars throughout the United Kingdom.

In the United States, Wimpy Grills languished. When Gold died in 1977, only six outlets remained. In the United

Kingdom, on the other hand, the Wimpy chain did well and hundreds of outlets were opened. McDonald's opened its first restaurant in London in 1974. Wimpy began advertising extensively, including, in 1976, on children's television. But McDonald's rapidly expanded throughout the UK, and by the end of the century had more than 1,000 outlets throughout the British Isles.

Faced with heavy competition from McDonald's, Lyons sold the UK Wimpy outlets to United Biscuits, who in turn sold them to Grand Metropolitan. Subsequently, Grand Metropolitan acquired Pillsbury, which owned Burger King. Grand Metropolitan concluded that Burger King was a more efficient operation and it converted many Wimpy Bars into Burger King restaurants. By 1998 Wimpy's franchises had declined to 280 counter-service outlets in the UK. In 2002, investors acquired Wimpy International. Despite the changes in ownership, Wimpy has continued to innovate on its menu. The 'Beanburger' was introduced in 1987, and the Quorn Burger, a vegetarian alternative to the hamburger, in 1997. Competition from McDonald's and other fast-food chains has greatly diminished the number of Wimpy outlets, but the company is the oldest surviving hamburger chain in the United Kingdom.

In 1958, Gold and Lyons created Wimpy International to promote the chain outside the United States and the United Kingdom. During the following decades, Wimpy outlets were opened in other countries, but its greatest success outside the US and the UK was in South Africa, where the company opened its first outlet in Durban in 1967. The chain has thrived in South Africa ever since.

The success of Wimpy, and later McDonald's and Burger King, in the United Kingdom encouraged the growth of indigenous hamburger chains. In 1958, Sam Alper opened the first Little Chef restaurant in Reading. Specializing in beefburgers, the chain slowly expanded and its ownership changed hands several times. In 1996, Granada, the broadcasting conglomerate, acquired the Little Chef chain. Happy Eater, a chain of roadside restaurants, was launched in 1973 by Michael Pickard. Within seven years, the firm had 21 restaurants, at which point it was taken over by Imperial Group PLC. Granada acquired the Happy Eater chain in 1995. Two years later, the Happy Eaters were converted into Burger Kings and Little Chefs. Due to stiff competition and lack of renovation, many Little Chef restaurants have closed.

Another chain, Gourmet Burger Kitchen, was launched by chef Peter Gordon and two other New Zealanders in the south of England in 2001. Gourmet Burger Kitchen claims to use the most nutritious products with the freshest ingredients available. They offer a hamburger made from Aberdeen-Angus Scotch beef combined with other ingredients such as cheddar, Stilton, mozzarella or blue cheese, garlic mayonnaise and numerous sauces – satay, chilli, barbecue, mango and ginger. Some other condiments that may be added are pesto, beetroot, egg, pineapple, avocado and bacon. They also serve a 'Kiwi Xmas Burger' composed of turkey, ham, avocado and kiwifruit salsa, and a 'Brit Xmas Burger' with turkey, stuffing, bacon and cranberry sauce.

Other burger chains that have developed in the United Kingdom include Fine Burger Company, Real Burger World, Ultimate Burger and Hamburger Union, which claims that its burgers are 'handmade on the premises from meats which are naturally reared, grass fed or free range and cooked on a chargrill'.

Europe

American fast-food chains have opened outlets in virtually every European nation. McDonald's alone has more than 6,000 outlets in 41 European nations. These outlets have inspired the creation of local hamburger chains. Bicky Burger is sold at many outlets in the Netherlands. The Burghy hamburger chain was launched in Milan in 1982. When McDonald's had difficulty establishing itself in Italy, it purchased the Burghy chain in 1996. Harold's Hamburger Snack Bar opened in Geneva, Switzerland in 1975. Its speciality was the HaroldBurger, made from a quarter pound of fresh ground beef with slices of cucumbers, onions and tomatoes; another unusual burger is the BlueBurger made from a mixture of ground beef and blue cheese. In the Netherlands, hamburgers have become so common that they are sold in vending machines.

After World War II, southern Germany was occupied by American military forces and it soon became one of the first European nations to be targeted by American fast-food chains. A&W Root Beer opened an outlet in Germany in 1962, followed by McDonald's in 1971. When the Berlin Wall fell in 1989, McDonald's rushed into the former East Germany. McDonald's has co-branded with Wal-Mart and has outlets in Wal-Mart stores in Germany. Germany has become one of the company's most successful markets, using only German potatoes and beef.

In 1972 McDonald's opened its first restaurant in France. By 1988 McDonald's had established itself as one of France's most popular fast-food operations. Today, more than 1,000 McDonald's outlets are located throughout France. Burger King fared less well: having opened its first operation in the early 1980s, it closed all 39 of its French operations in 1998.

Hamburger vending machines in Amsterdam, The Netherlands.

McDonald's opened its first restaurant in Moscow in 1990, and the company has expanded slowly in Eastern Europe. The world's largest McDonald's operates near Red Square in Moscow. When it opened, a Big Mac lunch cost the equivalent of a week's wages. Today, one McDonald's in Russia serves 40,000 people every day.

Asia

In contrast to its rapid integration into European diets, American fast-food fare could not be absorbed easily into the cuisines of East Asia. Japan, however, was occupied by American armed forces, making it relatively easy for American fast-food operations to open there. The first McDonald's opened in Tokyo in 1971, and is today the most popular restaurant in Japan, measured by volume of customers. As of 2005, McDonald's operated 3,800 branches across Japan.

The success of McDonald's in Japan encouraged the growth of non-American-owned chains. MOS Burger (the first

McDonald's has thrived outside the United States. This McDonald's is located in Osaka, Japan, 2007.

word is an acronym of 'Mountain Ocean Sun') was launched the year after McDonald's opened its first Japanese outlet. According to Katarzyna J. Cwiertka's book, *Modern Japanese Cuisine*, the founders of MOS Burger made a careful study of how McDonald's was run – and then did the exact opposite. Instead of cranking out quick, cheap hamburgers, MOS Burger emphasized the quality and safety of its ingredients. This strategy was successful: the company opened its first outlet in 1972 and, by 1998, had 1,500 outlets. MOS Burger has been extremely innovative in the products on offer: a Teriyaki Burger, introduced in 1973, has become a standard item on the

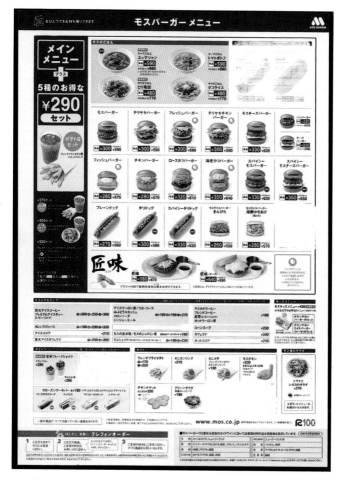

MOS Burger opened up a year after McDonald's opened its first franchise in Japan. Its menu included many different types of hamburgers.

Inside a MOS Burger stand at Nara, Japan.

menu of all hamburger chains in Japan. Later, MOS Burger introduced the Rice Burger and the Japanese Burger, 'Takumi Judan', a beef patty topped with a fried egg and bacon.

Other indigenous Japanese hamburger chains include Lotteria and Freshness Burger. Lotteria opened its first outlet in 1972. Unlike MOS Burger, Lotteria followed the McDonald's model, selling inexpensive hamburgers and other foods; however, in 1997 it began to expand its menu to include other types of burgers such as teriyaki burgers and shrimp burgers. The company that became known as Freshness Burger was founded in 1981, but it did not open its first hamburger café until 1992. The company now has 250 shops throughout Japan, Korea and Hong Kong.

Thanks to the success of McDonald's and of Japan's own chains, other American hamburger chains have been less than successful penetrating the Japanese market. Burger King, for instance, opened its first outlet in Japan in 1996; five years later the company closed all its stores except those on US Air Force and Marine Corps bases. In cooperation with the Japanese-owned Lotteria hamburger chain, however, Burger King is again planning to open restaurants in Japan.

Like American hamburger chains, Japanese chains expanded to other countries. MOS Burger has outlets in China, Taiwan, Singapore, Hawaii and Hong Kong. Lotteria has opened outlets in South Korea, Taiwan, China and Vietnam. In South Korea, Lotteria has surpassed McDonald's as the most popular hamburger chain in the country. Lotteria's

Freshness Burger café, Osaka, Japan, 2007.

signature dish in Korea is Kimchi Burgers, in which the beef is mixed with pungent fermented cabbage, minced garlic and egg. South Korean Lotterias also sell other unusual items, including the Cheong-Yang Chilly Pepper Burger, the Paprika Bacon Beef Burger, the Korean Beef Bulgogi Burger and the Burning Squid Burger.

McDonald's opened its first outlet in South East Asia in 1979. It subsequently opened restaurants in Taiwan, Hong Kong, Korea and China. When McDonald's opened an outlet in Beijing, thousands of people queued for hours to eat there. As of 2005, McDonald's boasted more than 546 restaurants in China, and many more outlets were under construction throughout the country. Customers were attracted to McDonald's because of its uniformity and egalitarian atmosphere, but some of the McDonald's traditional models have been rejected in East Asia. For instance, the assumption that customers will eat and leave quickly doesn't seem to apply here – many consumers have concluded that the 'fast' in fast food refers to the serving of the food, not its consumption.

The hamburger was introduced into the Philippines by the Americans prior to World War II, but hamburger chains did not arrive until well after independence. McDonald's, called McDo by Filipinos, opened its first outlet in 1981 and was followed later by Burger King. Both companies sell burgers similar to those sold in the United States, but they are often accompanied by steamed rice. Local burger chains include the Jollibee, which started in 1975. Its signature burger is 'The Big Champ', a hamburger with everything on it. Jollibee is the largest fast-food chain in the Philippines, and has recently opened outlets in the United States and Hong Kong.

Unusually, the first burger chain in India was an indigenous company called Nirula's, which introduced fast-food burgers and chips during the 1950s. Menu items include the

Nutty Paneer Burger (made of fresh cheese and walnuts), Mutton Maniac Burger (with chilli sauce), French Flip Burger (a chicken burger) and Crazy Pea Burger (made from dried peas). Today, Nirula's is owned by a Malaysian equity company. McDonald's entered the Indian market in 1996 in cooperation with two Indian companies, Connaught Plaza Restaurants Pvt Ltd in northern India, and Hard Castle Restaurant Pvt Ltd in the western part of the country. Indian nationalist groups initially opposed McDonald's, and the company had problems selling its American products. To overcome this, local McDonald's franchisees developed the 'McAloo Tikki Burger', a patty of fried potatoes and peas flavoured with tomato, onion and spicy condiments. For the non-vegetarians, McDonald's created the 'Maharaja Mac', made with a chicken patty. In India, McDonald's uses Indian spices, and franchisees are careful to separate vegetarian and non-vegetarian utensils and products. Their buns are made from Indian-grown wheat. The McAloo Tikki Burger is the best-selling burger in India, and the Indian McDonald's restaurants are now exporting this burger to the Middle East, where it has become very popular.

McDonald's opened its first outlet in Pakistan in 1998 and, as of 2006, the company has eighteen outlets in the country. Burgers are also sold in traditional stalls near markets and shopping streets. The most famous burger is the 'Shami Burger', with a patty composed of lentil and minced lamb accompanied by toppings such as onions, scrambled egg and ketchup. McDonald's has more than 300 outlets in Malaysia, but there are also indigenous hamburger restaurants such as the 'Ramly Burger', which was launched in 1979. Its beef or chicken patties can be garnished with onions, eggs, cabbage, cheese, cucumbers, shredded carrots and the usual condiments.

In the Middle East, both McDonald's and Burger King have opened franchises in many countries, including Turkey, Jordan, United Arab Emirates, Qatar, Lebanon and Kuwait. In Saudi Arabia, hamburger chains follow halal dietary laws; in Israel, some are kosher, and many outlets do not serve cheese on their hamburgers. Burger King also operates outlets in Afghanistan and Iraq around American military bases. Johnny Rockets has restaurants in Bahrain, UAE, Qata, and Kuwait. Throughout the Middle East, burgers are sold on the streets by vendors as well as in fancy restaurants. Local hamburger chains, such as Lebanon's Juicy Burger, have emerged in some countries of the Middle East.

American hamburger franchises in the Middle East have had their ups and downs, according to political events. Shortly after the Iraq war in 1992, in which American-led military forces liberated Kuwait, McDonald's opened a restaurant in Kuwait, and the line of cars waiting to get in was seven miles long. In other Middle Eastern countries, American-associated hamburger outlets have been vandalized and firebombed. Fast food represents a lifestyle very different to that desired by many Muslims in the Middle East, as Benjamin R. Barber pointed out in his thoughtful *Jihad vs. McWorld* (1996).

Latin America and the Caribbean

American fast-food companies operate throughout Latin America and the Caribbean. In Mexico hamburgers are sold in American fast-food chains in major cities, but are also sold by indigenous establishments in remote corners of the nation. In Argentina, McDonald's and Burger King have a strong presence. These chains have encouraged the growth of indigenous hamburger chains, such as Carlitos de Gesell,

Hamburgers have reached every corner of the world, including the 'sleepy'
village of Mani, Yucatan, Mexico.

which sells a large variety of hamburgers. Argentina supplies
beef for hamburger outlets throughout the world. Argentin-
ean companies such as Quickfood and Finexcor (a subsidiary
of the US multinational Cargill) specialize in manufacturing
super-frozen hamburger patties of precisely uniform size,
weight and fat content. The vacuum-packed frozen patties
are shipped throughout the world.

McDonald's Comercio de Alimentos Ltda. (the subsidiary's official name) was launched in Brazil in 1971. By 2002
there were 619 kiosks and 572 restaurants in 21 of Brazil's 26
states, plus the Federal District. More than half are compa-
ny-owned; 142 franchisees own the rest. In 2001, an estimated
514 million people ate in a McDonald's restaurant somewhere
in Brazil. McDonald's is the nation's largest employer. A
chain called Bob's was launched by Bob Falkenburg, an
American tennis player, in 1951. Today it is the second largest
fast-food chain, after McDonald's, in Brazil, and Bob's has

begun operating in other countries. It serves a standard burger-and-fries menu, featuring an especially spiced hamburger, and milkshakes.

Africa

Africa, too, has seen some growth of fast-food hamburger chains. McDonald's opened its first African outlet in Casablanca, Morocco, in 1992. After the end of apartheid, a McDonald's opened in Johannesburg, South Africa. Local hamburger chains do well, too. South Africa's Steers restaurant chain, which sells hamburgers, is owned by Famous Brands, which also owns the Wimpy hamburger chain in South Africa. In Nigeria Mr. Bigg's, owned by conglomerate United African Company of Nigeria PLC, started up in the 1960s. It sells hamburgers, although the popular items are more closely connected with Nigerian culinary traditions. The second largest Nigerian fast-food chain, Tantalizers, opened in 1997, and sells a variety of hamburgers, along with meat pies, fried rice and chicken.

Globalization Problems

American hamburger chains rapidly expanded abroad during the 1970s, but they faced serious cultural barriers when they did so. In the States, it was understood that customers would queue to place their orders, which was not necessarily a tradition that existed in other countries. The McDonald's model was based on having customers pay before receiving their food which is, of course, quite the reverse from sitdown restaurants, even in the United States. American fast-food chains based their design on quick table turnover but in many other countries eating is not something to be accomplished at speed. James L. Watson, in his book *Golden Arches East: McDonald's in East Asia* (1997), points out numerous problems confronting McDonald's. Employees were trained to smile at customers – this is standard practice in the United States, but it raised suspicions in Moscow and China, where food service employees don't usually smile. Most first-time customers had no idea what a hamburger was or how it should be eaten. In most countries customers easily adapted to the McDonald's experience but there were places where McDonald's had to change its procedures to fit in with local customs.

Because of their rapid expansion around the world, American hamburger franchises are visible manifestations of globalization, which means that they are often targeted by those opposed to globalization or outraged by American policies. Demonstrators often ransack or destroy fast-food outlets around the world as a protest against American policy or against the whole concept of fast food. To avoid these problems, hamburger chains have done their best to localize their operations. Most fast-food chains are run and operated by local people. Chains make an effort to source a high percentage of their basic ingredients in the resident country, buying from local farmers when possible and importing ingredients only when necessary.

To avoid problematic culture clashes American-based hamburger chains have tried to fit in with the local ways of life. In India, you can order a veggie burger or a Chicken Maharaja burger. Pork products are not sold in Islamic nations. Beer is served at McDonald's in Germany, and wine in France. Espresso and salads are offered in Italy. McHuevos (poached eggs in buns) are sold in Uruguay. Frankfurters are offered in Germany. Vegetarian burgers are on the McDonald's menu in the Netherlands, and McLaks (salmon sandwiches) are offered in Norway. In Finland, the buns are made with dark, oval-shaped buns, which are made from rye flour rather than the usual wheat flour. Chilled yogurt drinks are offered in Turkey. Corn soup is sold in Taiwanese McDonald's restaurants. Teriyaki McBurgers are on the menu in Japan, Taiwan and Hong Kong, and Samurai Pork Burgers are served in Thailand. A burger with a fried egg, called the Kiwi Burger, is a big item in New Zealand. The McNifica, a hamburger sandwich with cheese, is on the menu in Argentina. The McPepper is sold in Singapore. In Athens, it's the Greek Mac, made with pitta bread, beef patties and a yogurt sauce.

Not all menu innovations have proved successful. In 2002, the McDonald's outlets in Norway released the Mc-Afrika, Burger which supposedly had a 'taste of Africa'. At the time, southern Africa was in the grip of disasters – heavy floods, drought and starvation. Protesters complained that McDonald's should not be profiting from a name when there were millions of people starving.

It isn't just the menus that have been localized, but also procedures. Hamburger franchises outside the United States do not necessarily follow the standard American fast-food pattern. In Rio de Janeiro waiters serve hamburgers with champagne in candle-lit restaurants; in Caracas hostesses seat customers, take orders and deliver meals; and at peak hours in Korean McDonald's outlets, employees seat customers at tables already occupied by others.

There are many reasons for the success of fast-food chains in other countries. Most have adapted to foreign cultures, including revising the ingredients in their burgers. In addition to friendly, efficient service and good food, other factors contributing to their success are cleanliness, a family atmosphere, bathrooms and air-conditioning.

Despite the rapid success of hamburger enterprises throughout the world, there has been heated criticism of their effects on local cultures and businesses. Serious nutritional, environmental and cultural questions about fast food remain. As the homogenization of food choices continues worldwide, some consider the rapid expansion of fast-food chains an example of insidious American imperialism that is destroying local cultures and culinary values.

When the first McDonald's restaurant opened in Rome, demonstrations and concerns were expressed about the Americanization of Italian food. Carlo Petrini, a Marxist journalist from north-west Italy, believed that the industrialization of food was standardizing taste and leading to the loss of thousands of local and regional foods. In 1986 he met with 61 others in Barolo, Italy, to create Arcigola. Three years later, Arcigola evolved into Slow Food International. Its headquarters is now located in Bra, Italy. Its major publication is *Slow: The International Herald of Tastes; The Magazine of the Slow Food Movement*. Today, Slow Food is active in 50 countries and has a worldwide membership of more than 80,000. Slow Food USA, a non-profit educational organization with 12,000 members, is divided into 140 local 'Convivums'. It is dedicated to preserving endangered eating habits, celebrating local food traditions, such as animal breeds and heirloom varieties of fruits and vegetables, and promoting artisan products. It advocates economic sustainability and biodiversity through educational events and public outreach programmes.

A French cheese maker, José Bové, became upset with US tariffs on the importation of Roquefort cheese that were imposed in response to the European Union's refusal to permit the importation of American beef. He and his group, the radical Confederation Paysanne, decided to retaliate by bulldozing a local McDonald's restaurant under construction in the French town of Millau. Bové presented his action as a challenge to globalization. When he went on trial, 30,000 of his supporters demonstrated outside the court carrying signs reading 'Non à McMerde'. Bové was convicted of criminal vandalism and served three months in a French prison. Subsequently, he and his supporters destroyed research plots where genetically modified crops were being tested in Brazil, and have participated in demonstrations (some of which have turned violent) against globalization.

It addition to violent protests against globalization, hamburger chains have been subject to violence related to other international events and causes. In 1979 Marxist guerrillas blew up a McDonald's outlet in San Salvador, proclaiming their act a blow against 'imperialist America'. When American aircraft accidentally bombed the Chinese Embassy in Belgrade during the war in Yugoslavia in 1999, Chinese students ransacked the McDonald's in Beijing. Anarchists destroyed a McDonald's in Copenhagen and they regularly protest at the McDonald's outlets in Paris and London. Bombs have destroyed McDonald's restaurants in St Petersburg, Athens and Rio de Janeiro. Vegetarians have set fire to a McDonald's in Antwerp, and a McDonald's in London has been vandalized. In 2000 a bomb was set off in a McDonald's restaurant in Brittany, France, killing a 27-year-old employee; five activists belonging to Emgann, a group seen as a front for the Breton Revolutionary Army, were arrested. As previously mentioned, in 2001 500 enraged Hindus ransacked a McDonald's in Bombay, India, and smeared cow dung all over a statue of Ronald McDonald, because they thought the French fries served at the restaurant were being fried in beef tallow (which wasn't true). In 2002 the McDonald's in Bali, Indonesia, was bombed by Indonesian terrorists. When American troops attacked Iraq in 2003 protests were held in many cities, and again McDonald's was a target of demonstrations. In Moscow, a McDonald's restaurant was destroyed by a bomb.

Yet another cause of violence has been crime. In 2001 a bomb was set off in a McDonald's restaurant in Xian, China, killing two people. Two years later, a man was convicted of the bombing – prior to the attack, he had sent the management threatening letters requesting money.

Global Success

In the United States hamburger chains are now considered a mature industry. As the American culinary scene has grown more competitive, profits per outlet have declined. Major fast-food chains have looked to other countries for growth. Despite problems, American hamburger chains have enjoyed phenomenal success around the world. They appeal particularly to the busy, upwardly mobile middle classes in other countries. Customers are attracted to their efficiency, reliability, predictability, cleanliness – and public toilets. In many countries, American-style hamburgers are cheaper than other casual dining options. Finally, customers flock to American fast food simply because it is American. Considered exotic when they first appear, American fast-food outlets soon come to symbolize safety, convenience, fun, familiarity, sanctuary, modernity and connectedness to the world.

To many people throughout the world, American fast food represents affluence and innovation and reflects what is considered by many to be 'the good life'. To critics, these same chains represent the bloated lifestyle in the United States and the American cultural domination of the world.

7

Hamburgers Today and Tomorrow

The application of efficiency to food production has greatly changed what Americans eat and how Americans live. But before there were drive-through windows, there were cars. Early twentieth-century efficiency guru Henry Ford figured out that if he could build automobiles efficiently, he could sell them cheaply, making his profits on volume rather than on each individual car. In 1913, to keep costs down, Ford installed moving assembly lines to build Model Ts. While each worker's tasks were repetitive and boring, Ford paid his workers a comparatively decent wage for the time, and he stressed a lifelong commitment to his company. Launched in 1916, White Castle applied Ford's principles to serve up inexpensive hamburgers and make a profit by increasing the volume of their sales. Like Ford, White Castle set up a fund for major medical expenses for the company's employees and their families and developed a profit-sharing system with cash bonuses.

Efficiency was an important part of the McDonald's model, called the Speedee Service System. Richard and Maurice McDonald carefully eliminated unnecessary steps in making and packing hamburgers, French fries and beverages. They acquired the most up-to-date time-saving equipment,

Hamburgers became a social icon during the 1960s, and hamburger images appeared on all sorts of ephemera, including T-shirts.

and designed the kitchen for maximum efficiency. But the brothers did not follow Ford's model when it came to staffing: McDonald's employees were paid minimum wages with no benefits. The system developed by the brothers was refined by McDonald's and other chains over the next 50 years.

Today, most fast-food chains and many full-service restaurants use frozen foods – hamburger patties, chicken, taco meat, buns and potatoes. Some chains actually use conveyor belts and assembly lines to ensure standardization. Employees clad in identical uniforms are trained to greet customers in the same specific way. The kitchens are filled with buzzers and flashing lights that tell employees what to do. The computerized cash registers issue their own commands.

Fast-food companies buy in such volume that they can demand anything they want from suppliers, and bargain for lower prices. To fulfil contracts with fast-food chains, suppliers have reduced employee wages and, many say, have lowered their health and safety standards as well.

George Ritzer, author of *The McDonaldization of Society* (1996), has argued that the fast-food industry has promoted efficiency over other important human values. The industry's striving toward efficiency, according to Ritzer, has homogenized American life – and, thanks to the globalization of fast food, it is now homogenizing the lives of people around the world.

Build a Better Burger

In addition to academic interest, the hamburger has also become a part of pop culture. Artists such as Claes Oldenburg and Andy Warhol ate hamburgers as well as using them as subject matters for their works. Oldenberg's *Hamburger, Two Cheeseburgers with Everything* and *Floor Burger* and Warhol's *Hamburger* and *Double Hamburger* became popular images throughout America. The ubiquitous hamburger has appeared on T-shirts and provided the basis for every sort of ephemera from ashtrays to a batmobile motorcycle constructed in the shape of a hamburger. Hamburgers have starred in television series such as the *Jetsons* and *American Dad*, and in films, such as *Moscow on the Hudson*, starring Robin Williams. McDonald's and other well-known hamburger chains have appeared in numerous movies. When actors are not eating burgers on camera, they have been photographed eating them on the set: one such photographed featured Jimmy Lyndon and Elizabeth Taylor, who were filming for

Andy Warhol's *Four Hamburgers*, c. 1985–6, synthetic polymer paint and silkscreen ink on canvas.

Pop artist Claes Oldenburg used hamburgers as a subject for several of his works, including *Two Cheeseburgers with Everything (Dual Hamburgers)*, canvas filled with foam rubber and cardboard boxes, painted with latex and Liquitex, 1962.

Hamburgers appeared in the episode titled 'Homeland Insecurity' in the television series *American Dad*, 2005.

Hamburgers were so commonplace in America that they frequently appeared in television serials, such as *The Jetsons*, 1962–87.

The film *Cynthia*, starring Jimmy Lyndon and Elizabeth Taylor, was not popular with their fans, but they did enjoy a hamburger on the set in 1947.

The Jackson Five (Randy Jackson, Marlon Jackson, Jackie Jackson, Tito Jackson and Michael Jackson), photographed with Mackenzie Phillips on a hamburger in 1976–7.

'Sgt. Pepper's Lonely Hearts Club Band', Barry Gibb, Maurice Gibb, George Burns, Peter Frampton and Robin Gibb also appeared with a large, dripping hamburger in 1978.

Cynthia. As hamburgers are so 'American', virtually every politician running for office wants to be photographed eating one, Hillary Clinton being one such example. Large hamburgers have also provided the backdrop for musical groups and musicians, such as the Jackson Five. Hamburgers have become so popular that soft drinks companies, such as Coca-Cola, have advertised their products along with visual images of hamburgers.

Numerous chefs have claimed to have prepared the 'world's largest hamburger'. Others have tried to improve the hamburger through competition. The most famous effort is the Food Network's 'Build a Better Burger National Cook-Off', which is sponsored by the Sutter Home, a winery in St Helena, California. Since 1990 the contest has encouraged burger innovation and creativity. There are traditional 'beef burger' and 'alternative burger' divisions.

While running for office in the United States, candidates will usually be photographed eating hamburgers. Here, Hillary Clinton, candidate for the Democratic nomination for President, stops for a bite in Iowa on 8 October 2007.

The above is claimed to be the world's biggest hamburger, New Jersey, America, 17 December 2006.

Coca-Cola advertisement promoting its linkage with hamburgers.

Contestants have used a wide range of unusual ingredients, including Thai peanut pesto, tamarind sauce, spinach, avocado sauce, pineapple, pistachio nuts, goat's cheese, coleslaw, shrimp, cranberries and pecans. In 2004, the Grand Prize was set at $50,000, making the Build a Better Burger

National Cook-Off one of the top five highest-paying cooking contests in America. The 2006 winner, Camilla Saulsbury, a sociology professor, presented her 'Born in Berkeley Burger', which was a bacon cheeseburger with aged Teleme cheese, an arugula-fig topping, pepper bacon and fennel. The first runner-up was Jenny Flake of Gilbert, Arizona, whose 'Feta Florentine Burger' was served with prosciutto on a Parmesan-toasted ciabatta roll.

The World's Most Expensive Hamburger

Hamburgers have gone through a series of changes over the past several decades. For more than a century they had been a working-class and middle-class food, promoted and sold by street vendors and drive-in chains, but in the late twentieth century hamburgers entered the realm of haute cuisine.

In 1975, New York's famous '21' Club introduced the '21 Burger', priced at $21. It was served 'nude' – without a bun. Burger connoisseurs pronounced it 'the best burger in the world' and it was undoubtedly the most expensive in the world at that time. In New York City in 2001, four-star chef Daniel Boulud opened DB Bistro Moderne, a more casual cousin to his elegant Restaurant Daniel. On the menu was the 'DB Hamburger', a ground sirloin patty stuffed with the rich, tender meat of beef short ribs as well as foie gras and truffles. At $29, it quickly became a smash hit, and the burger was featured in the *New York Times* and culinary magazines. It was as if the gauntlet had been thrown down, and other restaurateurs began to vie for the title of 'best burger' – and highest price.

In 2005 Miami's Prime 112 restaurant introduced a $30 Kobe-beef hamburger. In a somewhat less elegant setting,

Denny's Beer Barrel Pub in Clearfield, Pennsylvania, offered the 'Beer Barrel Belly Buster', made from more than 10 pounds (4.54 kg) of ground beef, 25 slices of cheese, lettuce, tomatoes, onions and a slathering of condiments on a sesame seed bun, which sold for $23.95 (but was later bumped up to $30). Marc Sherry, owner of New York's venerable Old Homestead Steakhouse, offered a $41 hamburger with Kobe beef, lobster, mushrooms and microgreens on a Parmesan twist roll. Daniel Boulud upped the ante by adding more truffle shavings and increasing the price of his hamburger to $50. The Burger Bar at Mandalay Place in Las Vegas offered the 'Rossini Burger', composed of Kobe beef, foie gras and truffles, for $60. (This was a take-off on *Tournedos Rossini,* a dish made with filet mignon, foie gras and truffles that was named for the nineteenth-century opera composer and epicure, Gioacchino Rossini.) Daniel Boulud retaliated with the DB Hamburger Royale with double truffles for $99. This culinary creation, served only during truffle season, won the *Guinness Book of Records* certificate for the most expensive commercial hamburger in the world.

However, in June 2006 the Old Homestead Steakhouse in Boca Raton, Florida, raised the stakes a tad when it unveiled 'the most decadent burger in the world', priced at $100. Made from a combination of American, Japanese and Argentinean beef, the burger is sautéed in grapeseed oil and garnished with organic greens, mushrooms and tomatoes. For each order, the Homestead Steakhouse makes a $10 donation to the Make a Wish Foundation. In 2005 the fashionable Zuma Restaurant in Knightsbridge, London, began serving a hamburger made with Kobe beef for $104. In 2006 both the Four Seasons restaurant in Jakarta, Indonesia, and the Estick restaurant in Madrid, Spain, added $110 hamburgers to their menu. When actor Pierce Brosnan dined with Rainer Becker, owner of the Zuma, the $134 hamburger, made from New Zealand Kobe beef, was created, and was subsequently offered on the menu. But then the Fleur de Lys restaurant in Las Vegas made a quantum leap by offering a $5000 hamburger with champagne. It comes with a certificate to prove that you have purchased it. Despite the quantum leap, hamburger aficionados are now predicting that even more expensive burgers will soon be marketed.

The Hamburger Tomorrow

The most world's expensive hamburger may help a restaurant gain visibility, but it is the common, inexpensive hamburger that is consumed around the world. It is cheap to make, easy to eat and infinitely variable in flavour, texture and presentation according to what kind of meat, additions, seasonings and condiments are used. It is this adaptability, constant innovation and systematic production that make it likely that in the future the large hamburger chains will continue to expand around the world.

Americans continue to eat hamburgers at home, as evidenced by the continually increasing sale of hamburger buns over the past two decades. They are frequently served at outdoor barbecues and picnics throughout the summer, especially on public holidays. The hamburger remains an important American culinary icon, and now, because of globalization and massive advertising, the hamburger has become a global staple.

In the United States, the restaurant hamburger's attraction continues to be its low cost, convenience and versatility: it's a quick and satisfying meal. To the traveller, hamburger chains offer a reassuring familiarity and uniformity. For those who make burgers at home, the hamburger's appeal lies in the ease and cheapness of its preparation and the appealing possibility of customizing it to the family's tastes.

During the past century, the hamburger sandwich has rapidly evolved, and it is likely to continue to do so in the future. Whether served in a restaurant, a fast-food outlet or the home, the hamburger is here to stay.

Recipes

Historical Recipes

To make Hamburgh Sausages

—from Hannah Glasse, *Art of Cookery Made Plain and Easy*, 1758

Take a pound of Beef, mince it very small, with half a Pound of the best Suet; then mix three Quarters of a Pound of Suet cut in large Pieces; then season it with Pepper, Cloves, Nutmeg, a great Quantity of Garlic cut small, some white Wine Vinegar, some Bay Salt, a Glass of red Wine, and one of Rum; mix all these very well together, then take the largest Gut you can find, stuff it very tight; then hang it up a Chimney, and smoke it with Saw-dust for a Week or ten Days; hang them in the Air, till they are dry, and they will keep a Year. They are very good boiled in Peas Porridge, and roasted with toasted Bread under it, or in an Amlet.

Beef Sandwich

—from Elizabeth S. Miller, *In the Kitchen*, 1875

Scrape one or two tablespoonfuls of raw beef from a choice, tender piece; season it with pepper and salt and spread it on a thin slice of bread, buttered or not, as preferred; fold the bread and cut off the crust, and divide in three pieces of uniform size.

Raw Beef Sandwiches

—from Mrs D. A. Lincoln, *Boston Cooking School Cook Book*, 1887

Scrape fine a small piece of fresh, juicy, tender, raw beef. Season highly with *salt* and *pepper*. Spread it on thin slices of bread, put them together like a sandwich, and cut into small squares or diamonds. This will often tempt a patient who could not otherwise take raw meat. The sandwiches are sometimes made more palatable by toasting them slightly.

Salisbury's Recipe

—from James H. Salisbury, *The Relation of Alimentation and Disease*, 1888

Eat the muscle pulp of lean beef made into cakes and broiled. This pulp should be as free as possible from connective or glue tissue, fat and cartilage. The 'American Chopper' answers very well for separating the connective tissue . . . The muscle should be scraped off with a spoon at intervals during chopping.

Simply press it sufficiently to hold together. Make the cakes from half an inch to an inch thick. Broil slowly and moderately well over a fire free from blaze and smoke. When cooked, put it on a hot plate and season to taste with butter, pepper and salt; also use either Worcestershire or Holford sauce, mustard, horseradish or lemon juice on the meat if desired.

Tartare Sandwiches

—from C. Herman Senn, *Recherché Side Dishes: Hors d'Oeuvres and Sandwiches*, circa 1901

Chop finely some lean cooked ham, also about a third the quantity of French Gherkins and a few capers. Mix them with a little stiff mayonnaise and tarragon vinegar. Spread the preparation between thinly cut slices of buttered bread, and make up into small sandwiches – diamond, finger, or oval shapes. Dish up and garnish with fan-shaped slices of gherkin and parsley.

Hamburger Steak Sandwich

—from Eva Greene Fuller, *The Up-to-date Sandwich Book; 555 Ways to Make a Sandwich*, 1927

Between thin lightly buttered slices of white bread place hamburger (chopped) steak that has been fried in butter until well done. Cover with another slice of bread. Press together and garnish with a pickle. Serve as soon as made.

Hamburger Sandwich

—from Florence A. Cowles, *Seven Hundred Sandwiches*, 1929

1 cup minced cooked hamburg
Hot tomato sauce
1 teaspoon minced parsley
1 teaspoon sweet green pepper
3 minced mushrooms

Mix all ingredients and place between slices of buttered bread. Dip each sandwich in a batter made of one egg, one cup milk, half a cup flour, and salt and pepper to taste. Brown in hot fat in frying pan. Serve with cole slaw.

Modern Recipes

Elegant Pan-fried Burgers

—Bonnie Tandy Leblang, an internationally syndicated food columnist, cookbook author and blogger, contributed this recipe. For more information, go to her website: www.biteofthebest.com

This recipe takes 7 minutes prep time, 12 minutes cooking time and makes 6 servings.

Necessities
Lean ground beef (1½ pounds [680 g])
Egg (1)
Scallions [spring onions] (4), minced
Beef or chicken broth (½ cup [120 ml])

On hand
Ketchup
Mustard
Dried thyme
Black pepper
Flour
Vegetable oil

Not so Necessary
Sliced mushrooms (10-ounce [280-g] package)
White wine (½ cup [110 ml])
Pita bread

How to: Combine beef, egg, 2 tablespoons ketchup, 1 tablespoon mustard, 1 teaspoon thyme, and some black pepper. Form into 6 patties; lightly sprinkle with flour, brushing off excess. Heat 2 teaspoons oil in skillet [frying pan], add and cook patties until desired doneness, about 3 to 5 minutes on each side. Set aside. Discard excess fat from pan. Add scallions and, if using, mushrooms; cook, while stirring, 1 minute until scallions soften, or 5 to 8 until mushrooms soften. Add broth or wine; cook while scraping up bits that adhered to pan. Stir in 1 tablespoon each ketchup and mustard. Pour sauce over patties. If desired, serve in pita, topped with sauce.

More time? Chill burgers for 10 minutes before cooking.
Go withs: Steamed fennel, green salad

Mini Turkey Burgers

— Source: Riki Senn, Viking Cooking School Corporate Curriculum Development Manager /Operations Director. Used with permission of the Viking Cooking School.

Burgers
⅓ cup [160 ml] part-skim ricotta cheese
¾ teaspoon kosher salt
½ teaspoon freshly ground black pepper
¼ teaspoon garlic powder
1 teaspoon Dijon mustard
1½ teaspoons Worcestershire sauce
16 ounces [450 g] ground turkey breast
2 teaspoons canola or grapeseed oil
8 dinner rolls or Parker House rolls, split like
hamburger buns

Optional Toppings
Cheese slices (such as cheddar, American or Monterey Jack)
Mustard
Ketchup
Mayonnaise
Lettuce

Tomato slices (use cherry tomatoes)
Pickle slices

Combine the ricotta, salt, pepper, garlic powder, Dijon and Worcestershire in a large mixing bowl and mix thoroughly. Add the ground turkey and mix gently with a large wooden spoon just until evenly combined. Note: Be careful not to over mix or the burgers will be tough!

Divide the turkey mixture evenly into 8 portions; gently roll each portion into a ball, then flatten each ball into a patty. Burgers should be about the same diameter as the dinner rolls.

Heat a large sauté pan or grill pan over medium heat.* Add the oil to the pan and gently tilt the pan to spread the oil evenly over the bottom; let the oil heat through.

Place the burgers in the pan in a single layer; they should not touch each other. Cook until the bottom of each burger is golden brown and crusty, about 3 to 4 minutes. Use a spatula to carefully turn the burgers. Cook until the second side is also golden brown and crusty, about 3 minutes.

Turn the heat to low and put a lid over the pan; the lid should not completely cover the pan, it should be half on and half off. Continue cooking the burgers until a meat thermometer registers 160°F [70°C] when inserted in the centre of a burger, about 3 more minutes. If making cheeseburgers, add the cheese slices in the last minute of cooking.

Remove the burgers from the pan and place each one on the bottom half of one of the rolls. Add your favourite toppings and the top of each roll. Serve immediately.

Makes 8 mini-burgers

*To cook the burgers on a grill, preheat a grill to medium heat. Clean the grates with a stiff brush, then oil thoroughly to prevent sticking. Put the burgers on the grill and cook until the bottoms are golden brown and crusty, about 4 to 5 minutes. Turn the burgers and continue to cook until the second side is also golden brown and crusty and a meat thermometer registers 160°F [70°C], about

5 minutes. If making cheeseburgers, add the cheese slices in the last minute of cooking.

Southwest Turkey Burgers

— Source: Barbara Pool Fenzl, author of *Seasonal Southwest Cooking*, winner of the 2005 best regional cooking book in the US (Gourmand Awards)

Ground turkey is healthier than ground beef and these burgers are so delicious you may never go back.

Makes 4 servings

1–1 ¼ pounds [450–550 g] ground turkey
½ cup chopped green onion
1 tablespoon Southwest Spice Mix (see below)
1 tablespoon olive oil
4 large red onion slices, ½-inch thick each
Salt and freshly ground pepper to taste
4 slices Asadero cheese
4 hamburger buns, spilt in half horizontally
1 chipotle chilli in adobe sauce
½ cup [120 g] mayonnaise
1 avocado, peeled, pitted and thinly sliced
1 tomato, thinly sliced

In a medium bowl, mix together the turkey, green onions and spice mix. Form the mixture into 4 patties, about 1-inch thick. Preheat a barbecue grill. Oil both sides of each onion slice; salt and pepper to taste. When barbecue is hot put oiled onions and patties on the grill and cook until onions are tender and slightly charred, about 5 minutes per side. Remove from grill and set aside. Cook patties until cooked through, about 6 minutes per side. During the last minute of cooking, place a slice of cheese on each patty and continue cooking until cheese is melted. Open the buns and place them cut sides down on the grill; cook about

1 minute, until lightly browned and crisped.

In a small bowl, mix together the chipotle chilli and the mayonnaise. Spread about 1 tablespoon on one side of each bun. Top with a cooked patty, slices of avocado and tomato and cover with the other halves of the buns. Serve immediately.

Note: If there is any chipotle mayonnaise left over, use it to perk up a turkey sandwich.

Barbara's Southwest Spice Mix

I use this seasoning on everything – as a rub for chicken, seafood or poultry, sprinkled on tortilla chips before they're baked, tossed with vegetables and as a seasoning in dips or salad dressings.

1 tablespoon cumin seed
1 tablespoon coriander seed
1 tablespoon black peppercorns
2 tablespoons pure chilli powder
1 teaspoon sugar
1 teaspoon salt
½ teaspoon cayenne pepper

Heat a small skillet [frying pan] over medium heat; add cumin and coriander seeds and black peppercorns; cook until cumin is a shade darker and all of the spices give off their aromas, about 5 minutes. Put the toasted seeds in a spice grinder and pulse until finely ground. Transfer to a small bowl. Add the chilli powder, sugar, salt and cayenne and stir together well. Put in a glass jar with a tightly fitting lid and store at room temperature for up to one month.

Note: Pure chilli powder is simply a dried chilli ground up with no added spices or preservatives. It is available in speciality stores and through mail order catalogues. The chilli powder found in grocery stores usually has a number of other ingredients added – check the label.

Five Napkin Burger

— Source: Andy D'Amico, Executive Chef, Nice Matin in
New York City

The Five Napkin Burger was created for Nice Matin to satiate
that craving for comfort foods that we all have from time to time.
Of course it is not a dish that one expects to eat sitting along the
Promenade des Anglais, but we add the distinctively Provençal
aioli and a slice of French Comté cheese and it begins to make
sense for 79th & Amsterdam.

2½ lbs [1 kg] fresh ground chuck beef
4 hamburger rolls, preferably brioche
¼ lb [110 g] Comté cheese, sliced thin (substitute Gruyère)
1½ cups caramelized onions
1 cup aioli
4 slices ripe beefsteak tomatoes
4 leafs radicchio or bibb lettuce

Divide the meat into 4 equal portions and form each into a burger about 1 inch thick. Cook to desired doneness over a hot grill,
preheated iron skillet or under the broiler. Top each burger with
two slices of cheese and melt, place the burger on the bottom half
of a toasted bun. Top each burger with a generous portion of
onions and a heaping spoon of aioli (see below). Add lettuce and
tomato. Have 5 napkins at your disposal.

CARAMELIZED ONIONS

2 tablespoons olive oil
2 onions, thinly sliced
1 teaspoon thyme leaves
1 teaspoon salt
pepper

Heat the oil in a large skillet, add onions and salt, cook over low
heat for 45–60 minutes. Stir onions every 10 minutes, being careful

not to caramelize the onions too soon. After the onions have softened and turned golden, turn up the heat and cook until lightly
browned. Add the thyme, season with salt and pepper, cook 5 minutes longer and remove from heat.

AIOLI

2 large egg yolks
8 cloves garlic, crushed into a paste with a pinch of salt
1 cup [240 ml] olive oil
1 teaspoon fresh lemon juice
Salt and pepper

Whisk the egg yolks in a medium-sized stainless bowl until light in
colour. Add the garlic and begin to add the oil very slowly, in a thin
stream, while beating. As the emulsion forms, the oil may be added
faster. Add the lemon juice and season with salt and pepper.
Serves 4

Missouri Sirloin and Blue Cheese Burger

—Source: Bill Cardwell's 'Missouri Sirloin and Blue Cheese Burger'
in Marcel Desaulniers, *Burger Meisters: America's Best Chefs Give
Their Recipes for America's Best Burgers*, 1993

1½ pounds [680 g] lean ground beef sirloin
1 ounce [30 g] blue cheese
Salt and pepper to season
4 tablespoons unsalted butter, softened
4 1-ounce [30 g] slices white cheddar cheese
8 crisp slices smoked bacon
4 tablespoons spiced tomato relish, store-bought or
home made]

Gently form the ground beef into eight 3-ounce [90 g],
½-inch-thick patties.

Use a metal spoon to make a small, shallow indentation in the centre of four of the beef patties. Divide the blue cheese into four ¼-ounce [10 g] portions, and form the blue cheese into smooth, round balls. Place a blue cheese ball in each indentation. Top each with another patty, and gently form into burgers, making sure to seal all open edges. Season each burger with salt and pepper. Cover the burgers with plastic wrap and refrigerate until needed.

Grill the burgers over medium wood or charcoal fire. Cook to the desired doneness: 4 or 5 minutes on each side for rare, 6 to 7 minutes on each side for medium and 9 to 10 minutes on each side for well done. (This burger may also be cooked on a well-seasoned flat griddle or in a large non-stick sauté pan over medium-high heat. Cook for about the same amount of time as listed for grilling.)

Serve the burgers on toasted bread which has been spread with the softened butter. Top each burger with 1 slice of the cheddar, 2 slices of the bacon and 1 tablespoon Spiced Tomato Relish. Serve immediately, accompanied by additional Spiced Tomato Relish.

Vegetable Pan Burger

— Source: Michael Chiarello, Chef–Owner, Tra Vigne, St Helena, California, in Marcel Desaulniers, *Burger Meisters: America's Best Chefs Give Their Recipes for America's Best Burgers*, 1993

4 tablespoons extra-virgin olive oil
1 medium leek, white part only, cut into thin strips 2½ inches long
1 teaspoon minced garlic
½ pound [100 g] fresh wild mushrooms, stems trimmed or removed as necessary, sliced
Salt and freshly ground black pepper to season
1 tomato peeled, seeded and chopped
1 cup [65 g] shelled green peas, blanched

1 red bell pepper, toasted, skinned, seeded and cut into thin
strips
6 spinach leaves, stemmed, washed, dried and cut into thin
strips
2 tablespoons coarsely chopped fresh basil
1 teaspoon chopped fresh thyme
1 handful breadcrumbs
½ cup [50 g] grated Parmesan cheese
4 slices focaccia
4 1-ounce [30 g] slices fontina cheese

Heat the olive oil in a large non-stick sauté pan over medium heat. When hot, add the leek and garlic, and sauté for 1 minute. Increase the heat to medium-high, add the wild mushrooms, lightly season with salt and pepper, and sauté for 4 to 5 minutes. Add the tomatoes, lightly season with salt and pepper, and continue cooking until most of the liquid has evaporated, about 2 minutes. Add the peas, red bell pepper, spinach, basil and thyme. Stir constantly until heated through, about 2 minutes. Remove the vegetables to a 5-quart [5-litre] stainless-steel bowl and stir in the breadcrumbs and Parmesan. Adjust the seasoning with salt and pepper. Allow the mixture to cool to room temperature.

Preheat the oven to 375°F [190°C].

Gently form the vegetable mixture into four 6-ounce [170 g], 1-inch-thick burgers. Cover the burgers with plastic wrap and refrigerate until needed.

Toast the focaccia slices in the oven for 2 minutes. Spread the cut side of the focaccia with roasted garlic paste. Place a vegetable burger on each slice of focaccia. Place the burgers on a baking sheet, and top each burger with a slice of fontina. Bake until the cheese has melted and begins to brown and the burgers are heated through, about 16 to 18 minutes. Remove the burgers and focaccia from the oven and serve immediately.

Note: If fresh wild mushrooms are not available, an excellent substitution would be fresh shiitake mushrooms. Although these mushrooms are cultivated, they have a wonderful earthy flavour.

Two ounces [60 g] dried shiitake mushrooms that have been rehydrated in 1 quart [1 litre] warm water for 1 hour could also be used. Drain thoroughly before using.

Select Bibliography

Bloom, Emily, *Burgers Every Way: 100 Recipes Using Beef, Chicken, Turkey, Lamb, Fish and Vegetables* (New York, 2004)

Boas, Max, and Steve Chain, *Big Mac: The Unauthorized Story of McDonald's* (New York, 1977)

Décasy, Gyula, *Hamburger for America and the World: A Handbook of the Transworld Hamburger Culture*, vol. 3 of the Transworld Identity Series (Bloomington, IN, 1984)

Desaulniers, Marcel, *Burger Meisters: America's Best Chefs Give Their Recipes for America's Best Burgers, Plus the Fixin's* (London and New York, 1993)

—, *Burgers: Classic American Hamburgers and Their Accompaniments* (London, 1995)

Edge, John T., *Hamburgers & Fries: An American Story* (New York, 2005)

Graulich, David, *The Hamburger Companion: A Connoisseur's Guide to the Food We Love* (New York, 1999)

Hogan, David Gerard, *Selling 'em by the Sack: White Castle and the Creation of American Food* (New York, 1997)

Huddleston, Eugene L., 'A Burger Bibliography', *The Journal of American Culture*, 1 (1978), pp. 466–71

Kincheloe, Joe L., *The Sign of the Burger: McDonald's and the Culture of Power* (Philadelphia, PA, 2002)

Kroc, Ray, with Robert Anderson, *Grinding It Out: The Making of McDonald's* (Chicago, IL, 1977)

Love, John F., *McDonald's: Behind the Arches* (New York, 1986)

McDonald, Ronald L., *The Complete Hamburger: The History of America's Favorite Sandwich* (Secaucus, NJ, 1997)

Ozersky, Josh, *Hamburgers: A Cultural History* (New Haven, CT, 2008)

Petrini, Carlo, *Slow Food: The Case for Taste* (New York, 2003)

Rifkin, Jeremy, *Beyond Beef: The Rise and Fall of the Cattle Culture* (New York, 1992)

Rozin, Elisabeth, *The Primal Cheeseburger: A Generous Helping of Food History Served Up on a Bun* (New York, 1994)

Spurlock, Morgan, *Don't Eat this Book: Fast Food and the Supersizing of America* (New York, 2005)

Tennyson, Jeffrey, *Hamburger Heaven: The Illustrated History of the Hamburger* (New York, 1993)

Thomas, David R., *Dave's Way* (New York, 1991)

Websites and Associations

Hamburger History, Politics and Culture

McSpotlight
www.mcspotlight.org

Men Style, 20 Hamburgers You Must Eat Before You Die
men.style.com/gq/features/full?id=content_2526

National Cattlemen's Beef Association
www.beefusa.org/

What's Cooking America
whatscookingamerica.net/History/HamburgerHistory.htm

Wimpy's International
www.wimpy.uk.com/

Hamburger Restaurants

Big Boy Restaurants
www.bigboy.com

Burger Fuel
www.burgerfuel.com

Burger King
www.burgerking.com/bkglobal

Hungry Jack's
www.hungryjacks.com.au/

Jollibee
www.jollibee.com.ph

Lotteria
www.lotteria.com/

McDonald's
www.mcdonalds.com

Mos Burger
www.mos.co.jp/english/

Wendy's
www.wendys.com

Acknowledgements

I'd like to thank Barry Popik of Austin, Texas, for his research into hamburgers in the United States; Katarzyna J. Cwiertka, Centre for Japanese and Korean Studies, Universiteit Leiden, Netherlands, for her help with information about hamburgers in Japan and the use of two photographs from her book *Modern Japanese Cuisine; Food, Power and National Identity* (2006); Janet Clarkson of Brisbane, Queensland, for locating information about hamburgers in Australia; Ellen Steinberg of Forest Hills, Illinois, for finding and explaining nineteenth-century menus; Mark Zanger, culinary historian and author, Jamaica Plains, Massachusetts; Andy Coe, culinary historian and author, Brooklyn, New York, for locating early references to Hamburg steak; William Woys Weaver, food historian and author, Paoli, Pennsylvania; Wendy Woloson at the Library Company of Philadelphia for searching for information about Hamburg steak at the 1876 Philadelphia Centennial Exposition; and Judy Gerjuoy, who provided information about hamburgers in Finland.

Many friends contributed recipes. For the hamburger recipes, thanks to Bonnie Tandy Leblang, an internationally syndicated food columnist, cookbook author and blogger, who contributed the recipe 'Elegant Pan-fried Burgers'; Riki Senn, a member of the Viking Cooking School curriculum team, who contributed the recipe 'Mini Turkey Burgers'; Barbara Pool Fenzl, author of *Seasonal Southwest Cooking*, who contributed the recipes 'Southwest Turkey Burgers' and 'Barbara's Southwest Spice Mix'; and Andy

D'Amico, Executive Chef of Nice Matin in New York City, who contributed the recipe 'Five Napkin Burger'. Special thanks to Marcel Desaulniers, author of *Burger Meisters: America's Best Chefs Give their Recipes for America's Best Burgers, Plus the Fixin's*. Forty-seven prominent alumni of The Culinary Institute of America (CIA) contributed recipes for this book and the funds generated by its sale were contributed to the CIA. Recipes used from *Burger Meisters* are Bill Cardwell's 'Missouri Sirloin and Blue Cheese Burger' and Michael Chiarello's 'Vegetable Pan Burger'.

For the illustrations, special thanks to White Castle Systems International, Big Boy International and Richard J. S. Gutman, Director & Curator, Culinary Arts Museum at Johnson & Wales University, Providence, Rhode Island.

Photo Acknowledgements

The author and publishers wish to express their thanks to the below sources of illustrative material and/or permission to reproduce it. Locations of some artworks are also given below.

Photos courtesy of Big Boy Restaurants International: p. 72; © Robert Crumb, 1968: p. 62; photos courtesy of Richard J. S. Gutman: pp. 30 (top), 32 (top), 47, 74; photo Timo Jaakonaho/Rex Features: p. 95; photo © Paul Johnson/2008 iStock International Inc.: p. 6; photos courtesy of the Library of Congress, Washington, DC (Prints and Photographs Division, Office of War Information Photograph Collection): p. 8, 9, 21, 30 (foot), 32 (foot), 36, 38, 39, 43, 75; photos Everett Collection/courtesy Rex Features: p. 34, 49, 50, 54, 69, 115, 116, 117; photo Patrick Frilet/Rex Features: p. 103; photo David Howells/Rex Features: p. 118 (top); photos Michael Leaman/Reaktion Books: pp. 78, 96, 97, 98, 99, 112; photo *Milwaukee Journal Sentinel*/Wisconsin Historical Society/ Everett Collection/courtesy Rex Features: p. 22; The Museum of Modern Art, New York (Philip Johnson Fund, 1962): p. 114 (foot); © Claes Oldenburg 2008, courtesy The Oldenburg van Bruggen Foundation: p. 114 (foot); photo © Roger Viollet/courtesy of Rex Features: p. 37; photo Solent News/Rex Features p. 118 (foot); photo © The Andy Warhol Foundation for the Visual Arts/ARS, NY: p. 114 (top); photos courtesy of White Castle Systems International: pp. 26, 27, 29; photo © Wisconsin Historical Society/ Everett Collection/courtesy Rex Features: p. 52.

Index

italic numbers refer to illustrations; **bold** to recipes